tricks of the trade

From Best Intentions to Best In Show

by Pat Hastings
with Erin Ann Rouse

DOGFOLK
ENTERPRISES

Aloha, Oregon

Tricks of the Trade: From Best Intentions to Best In Show.

Text copyright © 2000 by Dogfolk Enterprises.
Illustrations copyright © 2000 by Karen McClelland.

Printed and bound in the United States of America. All rights reserved. No part of this book may be reproduced in any form or by any electronic or mechanical means without permission in writing from the publisher, except by a reviewer who may quote brief passages in a review.

Published by Dogfolk Enterprises, 17195 SW Division, Aloha, Oregon 97007, (503) 642-3585.

Cover by Bridget Backus McBride, Spotted Dog Creative
Cover Photos by Meg Callea

Interior Photos by Carl Lindemaier, Animal World Studio, and Libby Workman
Computer Illustrations and photo enhancements by Karen McClelland
Graphic design by Bridget Backus McBride, Spotted Dog Creative

Proofread by Judy Clover Schwabe
Printed by Bridgetown Printing, Portland, Oregon

Visit Dogfolk Enterprises on the Internet at www.dogfolk.com.

ISBN 0-9678414-0-2

For E. R. "Bob" Hastings

*Without you, I would not be offering the pearls
among these pages to others.
You taught me always to put the dog first,
to cherish my wonderment of puppies,
and to stay true to myself and my beliefs.*

*Thank You —
Your Wife*

*...and for Tinker, who taught me the secret of courage is
to take the journey together. You will always be with me.*

— Erin

*Great things are not accomplished by those who yield
to trends and fads and popular opinions....
They are accomplished by individuals who take untraveled roads.*

—Charles Kuralt

preface

This book is based on a seminar I give to dog clubs and other organizations within the Fancy. The seminar is geared toward the experienced dog person—breeder, exhibitor, and judge alike. However, on many occasions, these individuals have been accompanied to the seminar by a spouse or friend who loves dogs but is uninvolved in the sport. Of these people, many have come up to me at the end of the second day and expressed enthusiasm for the information being imparted. And then there are vets who have attended and expressed their appreciation for being able to extend their knowledge beyond medicine to the dog itself.

Like the seminar, this book was written primarily for the benefit of show-dog people. However, all of us who love, interact, or share our lives with dogs can learn from experience—our own or someone else's. With that in mind, I invite all dog lovers to peruse this book and glean from it ideas and approaches that might enrich your relationship with your favorite dogs. Whether we are breeders, exhibitors, or just people who get a kick out of dogs, these pages may have something useful to offer each and all.

I am reminded that everyone who is active in the sport of purebred dogs began as a pet owner. Whether we move on to conformation shows, obedience work, field trials, agility competitions, or simply neighborhood pet parties, our first best motive is love: for the eyes that watch our every move (especially at mealtime), for the tail that wags its overwhelming joy at our return, for the unconditional affection our dogs give without a moment's hesitation.

Dogs build their sense of security on routine and clarity of rules, but they thrive on a sense of purpose and challenge. They love being couch potatoes, but they are almost always ready for an Olympian sprint across a beach or field. They may shy away from a balloon or windup toy, but they are fearless if their loved ones are threatened. We have so much to offer each other. For our part, the offering comes from how much we are willing to learn for the benefit and welfare of our dogs.

I wish to extend my appreciation to all of those who came before us; to all of the authors from whom we have learned so much; to all of the veterinarians who have been willing to teach us, as well as learn from us; to the judges who have shared their insights and perceptions with us over so many years; and to our fellow handlers, exhibitors, and breeders who have always been willing to help make us better dog people.

More specifically, I extend my gratitude to Erin, for making me write this book (with her help); my brother, Tom, who told me I couldn't do it; my brother, Peter, who knows me better than that; and my brother, Fred, who has made us all better people; to Mike Billings, Edd and Irene Bivin, Ed Bracey, Dr. Lisa Branford, Marj Brooks, and Dr. Dan Buchwald; to Anne Rogers Clark, Lee Ann Clark, Dr. Hal Engle, Herman and Judy Fellton, Ed Gilbert, and Charlie Hamilton; to Lanny and Sabin Hamilton, Bill Holbrook, Ron and Laurie Lane, Dr. Jim Layman, and Karen McClelland; to Dr. Del Orchard, Dean Partridge, Lang Skarda, and Dr. Barclay Slocum; to my daughters, Audrey and Laurie Smay and my granddaughter Taisha Rae; to Cathy Spears, Patti Strand, Diane Vasey, Bob Waters, and Seymour Weiss. Each of you have helped to pave a way for the creation of this book.

As quoted by Mary Jane Hunt: "The moment of victory is much too short to live for that and nothing else." To all who have given me the benefit of their support, encouragement, experience and companionship, I thank you for making life so plentiful.

The quotes leading off each of the chapters to follow are some of my favorites from *The Road to Success Is Always Under Construction* (Larry Wall and Kathleen Russell) and *Think Big: A Think Collection* (Dr. Robert Anthony).

tricks of the trade

From Best Intentions to Best In Show

table of contents

INTRODUCTION XIII

1/ FIRST THINGS FIRST 17
    Kennel Leads 18
    Grooming Tables 18
    Grooming Arms 20

2/ PUPPY EVALUATIONS 23
    Process Parameters 24
    Evaluating for Decisions 32
    – Temperament 32
    – Head 33
    – Neck 36
    – Front Assembly 38
    – Depth of Chest 40
    – Length of Loin 41
    – Rear Assembly 41
    – Topline 45
    – Croup and Tailset 46
    – General Presentation 46
    – Substance 47
    Conclusion 47

3/ NUTRITION 49
    Food for Growing Puppies 49
    Dog Foods and Feeding 51
    A Healthy Weight 52

4/ TEACHING A DOG TO LEARN 55
    Interacting With Puppies 55
    Working With Dogs 57

5/ DOG WHEREWITHAL 65
    Puppies and Litters 65
    Raising Puppies 67
    Structural Review 68
    Caring for the Show Dog 73
    – Conditioning 73
    – Watering and Elimination 75

Table of Contents / TRICKS OF THE TRADE

  – Hot-Weather Protection 77
  – Crates and Air Travel 78
  – Collars and Leads 80
  – Bait 82
  – Honing the Show Attitude 84
  Miscellaneous Tips 85
  Tips for the Dog-Show Novice 91

6/ GROOMING FOR SHOW AND HEALTH 95
  Attention to the Basics 96
  – Nail Care 96
  – Bathing 98
  – Dryers 99
  Coat Care 99
  – About Dog Hair 100
  – Drop-Coated Breeds 101
  – Smooth-Coated Breeds 103
  – Spitz Breeds 104
  – Coated Breeds With a Jacket 105
  – Hard-Coated Breeds 107
  Scissoring 108
  Show Tips 109

7/ ADVERTISING DOGS 113
  Target the Audience 113
  The Advertising Budget 115
  Ad Layouts 115
  Ad Photos 116
  Attention to Strategy 117
  Recap 118

8/ THE BREEDER'S INTEGRITY 119

9/ AKC RULES AND PERSONAL INTEGRITY 125

RESOURCES 129

TABLE OF VISUALS 133

INDEX 137

*Where you come from isn't as important
as where you are going.*

introduction

My husband and I have worked and lived with dogs all our lives. We started as owners, got involved in breeding, and became professional handlers. Before we took on the awesome responsibility of living with and showing other people's dogs, we apprenticed for many years with professionals who taught us proper care, animal husbandry, and canine physiology.

My husband was an American Kennel Club (AKC) representative for five years, advising judges and exhibitors on show rules and regulations. We were both involved in obedience; Bob was part owner of an obedience school for a time. Early on, I was very active in 4-H dog events, helping youngsters to become good dog people. And throughout our careers, we were both active in kennel clubs, holding offices and working on committees. We have chaired all-breed shows and national-specialty shows. At this writing, I am an AKC judge, and Bob is an AKC judge emeritus.

We have taken many of the routes that one can take with dogs. We were very honored and fortunate to have shown great dogs. In our careers, we won over 250 Best in Shows, and we won Best in Shows from all groups. Between us, we have bred 28 different breeds; we've bred in every group. Even when we only bred a litter or two of a certain breed, we did so to learn more about the breed, because there is no better way to learn what a breed is all about than to have puppies, watch them grow up, and follow them through their lives.

I do not claim to be an expert on any particular aspect of dogs; I have no degrees connected with the dog world. This book is simply a compilation of what we have learned over years—and continue to learn.

Introduction / TRICKS OF THE TRADE

Your knowledge is only as broad as your exposure, and because of who we are and what we did, we had the opportunity to have a worldwide exposure that the average dog exhibitor never has a chance to experience. Also, we firmly believe that knowledge is wasted if it is not shared. So between our mentoring activities, my seminar, and this book, we are trying to give something back to the dog world—a world that has given us so much.

AKC is concentrating on judges' education and doing a fine job of it. However, AKC judges can only judge what exhibitors show, so we feel education needs to start with breeders. In the bygone days, there were large breeding kennels, complete with managers and private handlers. These kennels housed large numbers of brood bitches that could be bred to a considerable variety of studs in order to produce the strongest lines. This environment also developed dog people with a thorough knowledge of animal husbandry, defined best as the careful management of animals. And it made for skilled mentors from whom we could learn dogs from the ground up.

In today's world, there are very few large kennels and professional dog people; therefore, too many people are breeding dogs without fundamental dog knowledge.

A prime example is found in advertising. If breeders, exhibitors, handlers, and judges were universally well versed in structure and movement to the extent of having a full working knowledge of both, we would not see an abundance of poorly built dogs advertised—dogs that are winning as well as being used in breeding programs.

I sat down with several current dog magazines at our house one day and ended up with booklets of advertising photos that display dogs with serious structural and movement faults. With a basic knowledge of quality dogs, would owners, breeders, and handlers purposely publish photos of weak-structured dogs? Who knows if the poor quality is in the photo or in the dog, but what does it matter if what we see is an incorrect representation of the breed.

Everybody complains about "politics" in the sport of purebred dogs. However, it is more the perception of politics that is at work than the actual working of politics. As a professional handler, I knew there wasn't much politicking; as a judge, I have come to realize there is even less of it than I supposed as a handler.

The fundamental truth is that dog show judging is very subjective. What counts most (and what many exhibitors overlook) is the whole package. The best dog does not necessarily have the best chance of winning. The best package has the best chance, and the package has to include a quality dog that has been properly raised, conditioned, trained, groomed, and handled.

An AKC judge has 2.4 minutes to judge a dog. This includes paperwork, ribbons, and pictures. That leaves very little time for actual judging, so most dogs are judged on the immediate impression made by the dog-handler team.

In order to have the edge, you need a quality package. Winning is a matter of learning how to put the whole package together; that's what this book is all about. It's all hard work—there are no shortcuts. However, if you continue to do what you have always done, you'll continue to get what you have always gotten. If you aren't where you want to be in the sport, try something else—what have you got to lose? Don't be afraid to ask questions: There are no dumb questions when you're working to increase your knowledge base. Remember, education is the learning of all the things you didn't know that you didn't know.

What I will be discussing in this book are commonsense practices that have worked for us. They are not necessarily the only things that work, but they are approaches and, if you will, "tricks" with which we have had the best results.

As professional handlers, we went to an average of 100 shows per year and showed 15 to 20 dogs per show. This gave us the opportunity to have our hands on thousands of dogs. The ideas discussed in this book worked with almost all of the dogs we handled.

Be fair to yourself. Don't begin reading with the thought that your current approach is wrong. I simply offer some additional information to consider. There is no substitute for good breeding. However, it is entirely possible to ruin even the best-bred dog; it happens to the best-intentioned of us all. My hope is that this book will give you a greater edge on how to care for and enhance a showable dog, and possibly even how to enjoy your dogs more.

We all start in the same place, knowing absolutely nothing. We don't have to be in dogs very long before we think we know everything. As soon as we admit that such is probably not the case, we can begin again. From that point on, we find we are open to learning for the rest of our lives.

*If you can't find the time to do it right the first time,
when are you going to find the time to do it over?*

---

first things first

Showing dogs is one of the only sports in the world where everyone is on a level playing field. It makes no difference if you are an amateur or a professional, male or female, old or young. It does not matter what you do for a living or where you live. Everyone in dogs can accomplish exactly what they want to accomplish, as long as they are willing to do the necessary learning and work. And don't delude yourself with the excuse that it takes a fortune to succeed. If you are breeding and showing great dogs, the money will find you.

Although it may not cost big money to succeed in dogs, it does cost money. If you cannot afford proper equipment for your show dogs, you probably shouldn't be showing dogs. The array of equipment and supplies on the market is limitless. You don't have to buy it all; just learn how to spend your money on the things you really need. It is possible to succeed without spending a fortune.

There are three pieces of equipment that we feel are the most important tools you will own for all aspects of your life with show dogs:

1. One or several leather kennel leads.
2. A top-of-the-line, quality grooming table.
3. A sturdy grooming arm.

With these three tools, quality and durability are of paramount importance.

Chapter 1 / TRICKS OF THE TRADE

KENNEL LEADS

Leather kennel leads are difficult to find, but no serious dog fancier involved in anything other than toy breeds should be without one at every door and in every vehicle you own. It is the safest way to move a dog from one place to another—with something secure around its neck and your hand attached to it.

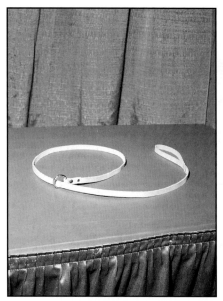

Figure 1-01: Kennel lead

Figure 1-02: Kennel lead in use

Because it is sometimes troublesome or inconvenient to put a collar and lead on or attach a lead to a collar, we can become very lax about doing it with each car ride or walk to the mailbox. A collar by itself is generally insufficient, as is leading a dog by its hair or ear. A leather kennel lead is easy and reduces unforeseen risks.

GROOMING TABLES

There are many types of grooming tables on the market, so make sure you do some homework before you buy. It is always better to purchase a table on sight instead of through a supply catalog, since pictures can be very deceiving. You need to see what you are getting—feel the weight (a consideration if you are going to cart it around to shows); check the welding and the edging. Make sure nothing is loose and no parts can develop instability with usage. Check with your hand to ensure there are no rough edges on which you or your dog can be injured.

For a quality table that will last a long time, the most important factor to consider is the height of the cross-member of the legs. The closer to the ground that beam is, the more stable the structure. Moreover, the less motion in a table, the longer it lasts—the lower the center of gravity, the less motion. Each time there is movement in the structure, the welding is compromised; thus, if the cross-member is high, the table will wear out much quicker.

Figure 1-03: High cross-beam

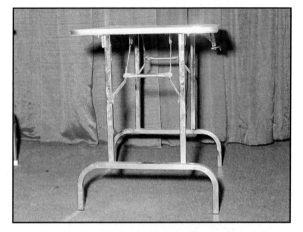

Figure 1-04: Low cross-beam

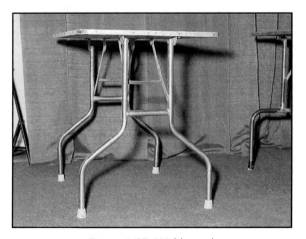

Figure 1-05: Wishbone legs

The shape of the table legs increases in importance with the size of the dog being worked. One common table leg used today is the wishbone shape. Although a table with wishbone legs is perfectly safe for small breeds, it can be a hazard for large breeds. If a large dog attempts to jump up from the side onto this kind of table or moves toward the side or edge while on it, the table could easily tip sideways. Whether the legs are square or round tubes seems to be irrelevant.

Another important quality to look for in a table is a nonskid surface. Keep in mind that the table is a tool not only for grooming but for teaching and molding. All show dogs should be taught confidence on a table; behavior patterns should be addressed on a table. However, any motion, any slickness to the surface on which a dog is being worked can potentially harm that dog's show career.

If the rubberized surface of a table is grooved with the length of the surface, it will not provide the dog sufficient traction. Make sure the grooves run with the width of the surface.

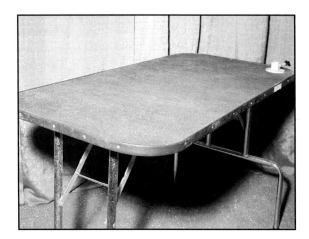 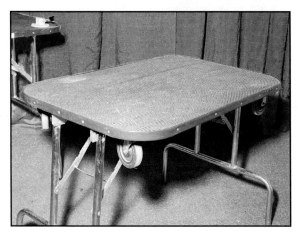

Figure 1-06: Correctly grooved surface   Figure 1-07: Incorrectly grooved surface

Also, avoid using tables with carpeted surfaces. Carpet offers inadequate traction, can create static in the dog's coat, and may disguise spills and accidents that can undo all of your hard work in a grooming session.

GROOMING ARMS

For a good grooming arm, look for a solid structure with as little motion as possible once it is in place, high or low. There are grooming arms available that are sturdy and hinged. This reduces the chance of bending or snapping, and you can move the overhang appendage of the arm out of the way, which simplifies matters if you are using the table for activities other than grooming.

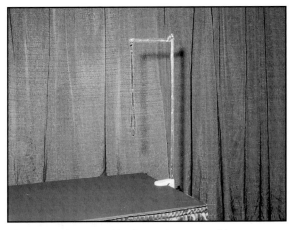

Figure 1-08: Grooming arm with appendage in place

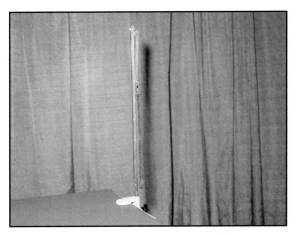

Figure 1-09: Grooming arm with appendage folded

With these three tools, take as few chances as possible. Buy quality, even if it means you have to spend a little more than anticipated. The return on your investment is worth it.

*Experience is a wonderful thing. It enables you
to recognize a mistake when you make it again.*

puppy evaluations

Mortality, by its very nature, suggests that all living things have in common a mix of strengths and weaknesses.

It follows, then, that the primary objective shared by all conscientious dog breeders is to improve the quality of their respective breeds. The goal is to breed for a perfect blend of:

- Type.
- Genetic integrity.
- Good temperament.
- Structural soundness.

Everything that you read and hear today about show dogs stresses type. Type is certainly the most important thing in the show ring; after all, type is what makes a specific breed. Type, however, must be taken within the context of the basics that comprise structural soundness. You have to have both type and structure to come up with a quality dog. Whether you are breeding or buying, it is of paramount importance to learn how to evaluate the structural quality of puppies.

Evaluating for temperament and structural soundness is a piece of the formula for success. You have to put it together with breed type, coat, colors, and the status of your breeding program. However, the formula is fundamentally flawed if it excludes the inborn composition of a dog's temperament and physical structure.

In this endeavor, there is no such thing as a "pick of the litter."

Frankly, the pick of a poor-quality litter is still poor quality. Although "pick of the litter" is a common phrase among dog people, we'd be wise to eliminate it from our mind-set and our vocabulary. What's required is to evaluate each puppy in relation to a standard of structural excellence and the breed standard, rather than evaluating it in relation to its littermates.

To assess breed type in puppies, study your breed standard carefully, bearing in mind what you need in your breeding program to improve type in your lines. To assess temperament and physical structure, the more advantages you have, the better—everything from a knowledge of canine anatomy and animal husbandry to an understanding of genetics and DNA testing. And, again, know your breed standard well.

We have used the process discussed in this chapter for several years. My husband and I evaluate an average of 250 litters per year, documenting each evaluation. As a result, we've been able to track the accuracy of our process, which continues to amaze even us. See what it can do for you and for your breeding program.

PROCESS PARAMETERS

As breeders, my husband and I made the same kinds of mistakes over the years that every breeder makes. We've all kept puppies we shouldn't have. We've all sold puppies we later wish we'd kept. And we've all placed some puppies with families whose lifestyles were incompatible with the puppies' capabilities. Throughout our involvement in breeding programs, we kept asking ourselves: What are we missing?

In our search for answers, we met with Dr. Hal Engle, head of the anatomy department at Oregon State University's School of Veterinary Medicine. The exchange of ideas at that meeting started us on a journey plotted by more and more questions.

Our research led us from one vet school to another, from general-practice vets to orthopedic surgeons, from research facilities to engineers. Each resource provided a piece of the puzzle; our challenge was to put that puzzle together.

The process parameters we recommend are as follows:

1. For structure, evaluate puppies only at eight weeks, give or take three days either way. This is crucial. Before eight weeks, soft tissue is not sufficiently developed to hold the bone structure in place.

As all bones grow at different rates, it is important to realize that the proportion of bone growth is as similar to the adult structure at eight weeks as it's ever going to be during the growth of the puppy. Therefore, what you see and, more importantly, what you feel at eight weeks is what the puppy will grow into as an adult dog.

This applies to all breeds across the board. The only exceptions we have found are premature puppies and puppies that have not had a good start. We've never had consistent results evaluating these two exceptions.

2. Evaluate the whole litter. Keep detailed records on every puppy in every litter you evaluate. You can then make the best possible breeding choices later on. It makes no difference if you recognize breed disqualifications or obvious pets among the puppies. Evaluate them all.

Understand that the real benefit of evaluating litters is education. The more breeders learn, the more their breeds benefit.

3. Keep a written record of each evaluation. Always record the results of each evaluation in writing. Then, when developing your breeding program, you will have not only pedigrees to consider but also the added advantage of written evaluation results. The more information you have, the better informed your breeding plans will be.

4. Select an objective grading system. We use a point system of 1 to 5: "5" being the best; "3" being an average dog of its breed that you see currently in the show ring; and "1" being the least desirable.

The reason for an objective grading system is to maintain focus on quality. It's so much easier to get where you want to be in dogs if you breed quality. Subjective grading encourages you to overlook structural weaknesses in favor of the puppy who captures your heart. Maybe its personality is just too cute, or maybe it possesses a single outstanding element you'd hoped the breeding would produce. But what about the puppy as a whole?

If you don't work to eliminate structural weaknesses from your breeding program, you will stand still and so will your breed. Produce quality dogs, then concentrate on type, coat, colors, and preferences.

The structural evaluation process is used to improve a breeding program, not to proclaim the arrival of the next record-breaking show dog. Bearing that in mind, our recommendation is: Any puppy that has any structural piece evaluated lower than average should be excluded from your breeding program.

If you see no improvement in structural quality and type from what you already have, don't keep any of that litter. If you want to be a top breeder, trying to represent a mediocre dog as great is self-defeating. Try again, and keep your sights on quality.

5. Evaluate puppies at a place completely unfamiliar to them. Puppies are too comfortable where they live. They need to be evaluated in a place where they've never been. Another room in your house doesn't count, because it all smells the same to puppies.

6. Have someone unfamiliar to the puppies handle them for the evaluation. The worst person to evaluate a litter for its structural quality is the breeder. It certainly can be done, but it's just human nature to try to make our "favorite" puppies look the best. The breeder may find subjectivity rules his or her evaluation findings. Basically, let someone working with a different breed evaluate your litters, and you evaluate theirs. That way, everyone learns. And it behooves us all to learn beyond our own breeds.

7. Evaluate puppies in a mirror. This is imperative to an objective review. Look at the picture in the mirror, not at the animal in your hands. A mirror provides distance; it gives you the opportunity to step away from the puppy, without ever having to step away from the puppy.

8. Let your fingertips be your best set of eyes. Your fingertips relay a great deal more information to your brain than your hands or your eyes do.

The most accurate view of a puppy's bone structure and tissue strength comes through tactile contact. Feel for skeletal formation, muscle mass, and motion as allowed by ligamentation. It's important to remember never to push past "the point of resistance" when feeling for motion.

Use "soft hands," fingertips, and gentle motions. You will be amazed how much you can see this way.

9. Be consistent in your evaluation steps. It is all too easy to let personal inclinations color the way we evaluate a litter. So in order to achieve the greatest possible accuracy, every puppy must be evaluated the same way, with as much objectivity as possible.

Attachments and preferences only hinder the benefits of the process. Handle each puppy the same way. Use the same procedure each time with each puppy. Concentrate on getting every puppy in as natural a position as possible.

Evaluate the entire litter, one puppy at a time. Resist the temptation to discuss your findings as you go. Once you have finished your evaluations and have recorded all of the grading, plus specific comments on temperament, testicles, mouths, balance, or whatever, determine and write down an overall score for each puppy.

THEN—and this is *very important*—go over the litter a second time to discuss each puppy. This time, take the puppies in reverse order, starting with the least-quality and working your way up to the best-quality puppy. This method will help you develop an eye for what is correct.

To evaluate for grading, we sugest the following procedure:

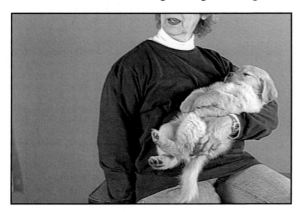

Figure 2-01: Correct hold for evaluating temperament

First, check **temperament**. To evaluate a puppy's temperament, turn it gently over on its back and cradle it in your arms and against your body. You want to give the puppy every opportunity to feel it's securely held, so that what you see is the puppy's genetic temperament traits, not a fear of falling.

Chapter 2 / TRICKS OF THE TRADE

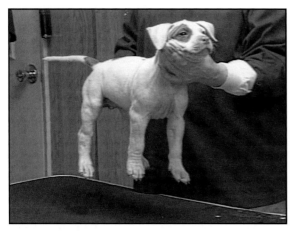

Next, look at the whole puppy in a **suspended position**. You need to position the puppy in such a way that it hangs free, without bearing any weight, and is completely relaxed. Pick a puppy up only on the bone structure of the skull, and between the rear legs—without touching the testicles, if it's a male. In this way, you won't influence anything the puppy's body does naturally.

Figure 2-02: Correct hold for suspended position

If you pick puppies up properly, they will relax and allow it. If you pick them up improperly, they either grab for your arm or fight you. Keep trying until you learn how to do this without stressing the puppy.

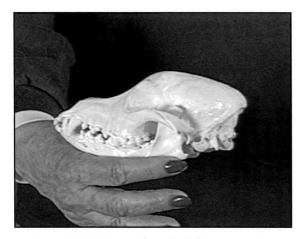

Figure 2-03: Correct front hold for suspending

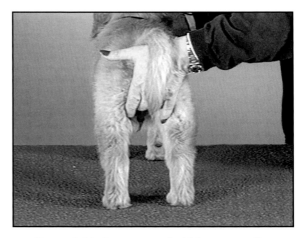

Figure 2-04: Correct rear hold for suspending

A well-structured puppy will hang in a very nearly stacked position. That is what you're looking for. If that isn't what you see, there is a structural reason.

PUPPY EVALUATIONS / Chapter 2

Figure 2-05: Suspended positionFigure 2-06: Standing position

Next, look at the whole puppy in a **standing position** on the table. Just try to make the puppies stand in a comfortable position. If they fidget, pick them up in the same fashion as you would for a suspended position, and run their feet along the table surface a couple of times. Puppies dislike the feel of a surface moving beneath their feet. Once you scrape their feet lightly across the table, they're usually so glad the table isn't moving anymore that they hold still.

After the puppy is standing comfortably and balanced on all four legs, the first thing you look at is the **overall balance**. Resist the temptation to fix the puppy. Just stack it in as natural a position as possible. Remember, the shape of the puppy at eight weeks is the shape it will grow back into as an adult.

Check the puppy's **proportions**, in accordance with your breed standard. In other words, check the height in relation to the length, and the depth of the body in relation to the height of the leg. Make sure you are following your breed standard, as some standards require the dog to be longer than it is tall, have a sloping topline, or so forth. (See Figures on page 30.)

Chapter 2 / TRICKS OF THE TRADE

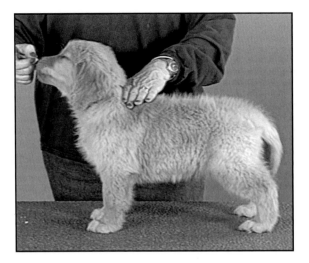

Figure 2-07: Check height at shoulder

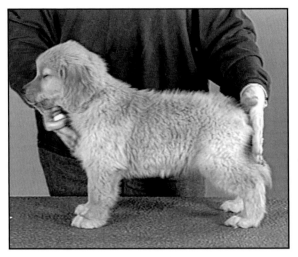

Figure 2-08: In relation to length of body

Figure 2-09: Check depth of body

Figure 2-10: In relation to height of leg

With the puppy comfortably stacked, look at the **whole picture**. Is there anything that stands out, such as a short neck, no front, or a lack of balance? Is the puppy correctly proportioned? If something doesn't look right, search for the cause as you go over each piece.

We go over a puppy in the following order:

1. Testicles.
2. Head.
3. Neck.
4. Shoulders.
5. Upper arm.
6. Elbows (for motion).
7. Front piece.
8. Front assembly angulation.
9. Depth of chest.
10. Underline.
11. Length of the rib cage & loin.
12. Hock angle and height.
13. Rear assembly proportions.
14. Fit of the knees.
15. Placement of the feet.
16. Shape of the pelvis.
17. Balance of muscle mass on the legs.
18. Hock stability.
19. Topline (standing & for motion).
20. Croup.
21. Tailset.
22. Bite.
23. Occlusion.

Last, but most certainly not least, evaluate the **nutritional effects** on structure. Position the puppy facing the mirror. Make sure the front legs are hanging free, without bearing any weight, and the puppy is completely relaxed. This shows you the true structure of the front legs. Gently lower the front feet back onto the table. If the front legs lose whatever soundness was seen while suspended, the problem usually is nutritional, not structural.

One thing we ask all breeders who bring us litters for evaluation is: What are you feeding the puppies? Almost all name-brand dog foods are top-quality products. However, we in the world of show dogs have a tendency to feed more than our puppies can utilize. Because of this, premium puppy foods that contain additional nutrients can allow the growth rate of bones to increase. Since there is no way to increase the growth rate of tissue, rapid bone growth can create structural problems.

Try to feed puppies according to their lifestyle. If they are confined to relatively small areas, they need only standard nutrients. The more activity and freedom they have, the more they are capable of handling additional nutrients.

Structural problems caused by nutrition are usually correctable by changing to a quality adult maintenance food. However, the change must be made before the growth plates close. After that, nutritionally generated structure problems are irreversible.

Finally, give all puppies the best possible chance at an objective evaluation. Work to keep them calm during the procedure.

Some people swing puppies in the air to calm them or act as though they were dropping them off the end of the table. However, both of these techniques generally produce the opposite results.

We use cheese during an evaluation—not as bait, but simply as a way to keep puppies' minds off what we're doing. Cheese is easy on their stomachs and keeps their interest. You don't want to use anything so enticing that you lose control.

Remember they're babies, not adult show dogs. You want to be as soft and gentle with them as possible.

EVALUATING FOR DECISIONS

In some respects, breeding dogs is a roll of the dice. Breed the best you have to the best you can, and you may still end up disappointed, having to let go of a whole litter and begin again. This is an inherent risk taken by even the most experienced dog breeders.

At the same time, making accurate decisions about each puppy's future can be equally difficult, unless you're measuring against a standard of excellence that includes a good temperament and structural soundness.

Temperament

When evaluating for temperament, you are looking for any one of four genetic temperament traits. Remember, this only works when the puppy is out of its familiar environment and being handled by a stranger.

1. Insecurity. A puppy that holds on is usually an insecure puppy. Insecurity manifests itself later as a dog more comfortable and at ease at home than elsewhere. For example, all of us have heard someone at one time or another say: "If the judge could come to my house, this dog would be finished." Such a dog is usually insecure.

2. Fear. A fearful puppy will open its eyes wide when you tip it down head first a bit in your arms. You will be able to see the whites of its eyes. You can actually see the fear. A fearful puppy may grow up with an exaggerated startle response and a greater fear of things. Many times, they are also sound-sensitive.

3. Aggression. An aggressive puppy will not let you hold it on its back, no matter how much you try to get it to relax.

4. Detachment. A puppy that will not meet your eyes usually will not form good human bonding. A "detached" puppy usually is very independent and marches to a different drummer. It makes neither a great show dog nor a great obedience dog. After all, if it won't form attachments with people, it certainly isn't going to try to please them.

When you identify any of these traits, socializing and exposure to a variety of positive experiences can help mask them, but the genetic causes of such traits will remain intact. Therefore, write down the traits you identify, then you will be aware of them if you use a puppy with any of these traits in your breeding program later on.

A sound temperament will show itself in puppies that are relaxed and confident that nothing is going to happen to them. That is the kind of temperament you are looking for.

Head

Evaluating the head is a very confusing proposition. This is a job for the breeder. When you look at the head of an eight-week-old puppy, if it's what you're looking for in an adult, then you need to find out if it's going to stay that way.

1. Head shape. In determining how the head will develop, you first want to evaluate the ridge, or zygomatic arch (or cheekbone), that runs between the eye and the ear, as well as the areas below and above that ridge. If the surface of the ridge is flat, and the areas below and above the ridge are fairly flush with it, then the back skull is most likely going to grow in proportion to what you are looking at. If the lateral surface is not flat, or the ridge is curved, the back skull will most likely broaden out of proportion.

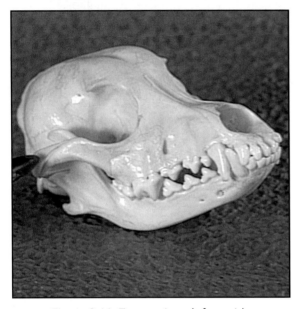

Figure 2-11: Zygomatic arch from side

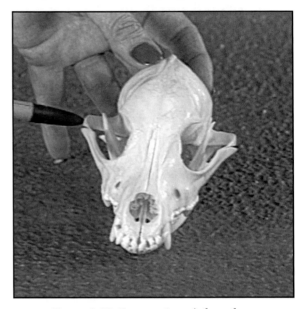

Figure 2-12: Zygomatic arch from front

The curvature of the ridge between the eye and the ear is made up of two bones. The strength of the muscle attachment on the head is what keeps those two bones from separating. The separation of those two bones allows the back skull to broaden. If there is a significant indentation above the ridge, the head will usually develop a dome shape.

If your evaluation indicates that the back skull will remain in proportion, ear placement and the shape and placement of the eye will remain proportionally the same as well. If the back skull broadens out of proportion, it can alter the shape and position of the eyes and the position of the ears.

2. Muzzle. In evaluating the head, the next feature to check for is a round, pellet-like formation on the skull bone, at the inside corner of the eye. It will feel like a small pearl. This round formation is part of the growth plate that controls the width of the muzzle as it grows. If that tiny ball is present, normally the muzzle will grow forward, in proportion to what you're looking at. If it is absent, and you feel a small indentation instead of a tiny ball, the muzzle will probably narrow.

3. Bite and occlusion. When looking at the mouth, the bite needs to be what your breed standard calls for, but don't stop there. Check the placement of all four canines, and check for proper occlusion on the sides.

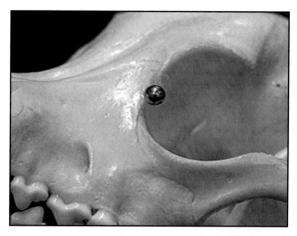

Figure 2-13: Simulated growth plate at inside corner of eye

The side teeth fit together like cogs of a wheel, or teeth on a pair of pinking shears. If they're misaligned, the mouth can change well into adulthood. This is one of the reasons why good mouths can go bad.

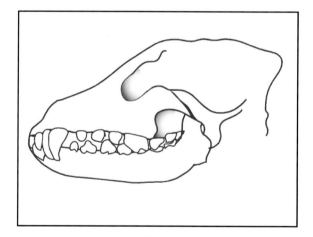

Figure 2-14: Proper occlusion

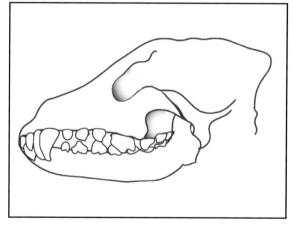

Figure 2-15: Improper occlusion

If there appears to be a problem with the alignment of the canines, talk to a dental vet about interceptive orthodontics–a perfectly legal option, when dealing with puppy teeth. According to one report, interceptive orthodontics is effective in 50 percent of all cases.

Neck

In most breeds, the neck is of paramount importance in detecting front assembly problems. If you were to draw a line along the puppy's topline, its head should be well above that line. If it isn't, the puppy has a short neck, which almost always indicates something is not quite right with the front.

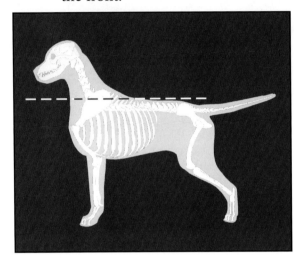

Figure 2-16: Good neck   Figure 2-17: Short neck

One possible cause of a short neck is a poorly placed front assembly, which is a very common problem in the dog world today. All dogs have seven vertebrae in their necks; however, an improper placement of the front assembly can cause an X-ray to show only five or six. This is because the shoulder blade itself is actually hiding one or more of the vertebrae.

One way to verify a poorly placed front assembly is by the elbows. Place your left hand under the chest and with your index finger and thumb on the elbows, squeeze them together just until you feel resistance. If the elbows come together, the placement of the front assembly is the problem.

In such a case, the reason you can move the elbows is because the upper arm is in front of the rib cage, instead of alongside the rib cage. This causes a sloppy upper arm movement instead of a good, strong forward action.

PUPPY EVALUATIONS / Chapter 2

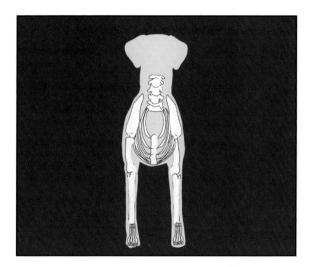

Figure 2-18: Good front assembly

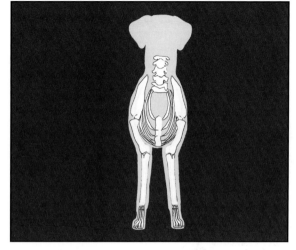

Figure 2-19: Poor front assembly

Another cause of a short neck could be straight shoulders, which we'll discuss in "Front Assembly." What matters is that a dog with a short neck—whatever the cause—will almost always have less reach, because a dog usually can only reach to the end of its nose, so the shorter the neck, the shorter the reach.

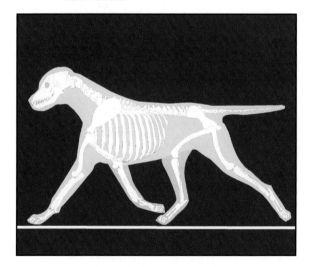

Figure 2-20: Good reach

Figure 2-21: Short reach

Chapter 2 / TRICKS OF THE TRADE

Figure 2-22: Good neck

Figure 2-23: Ewe neck

If you can gently tip the puppy's head all the way back to the shoulders, the puppy probably has a ewe neck. A dog with a ewe neck can compensate for this structural weakness by tucking its head into its body, thus giving the appearance of a short neck.

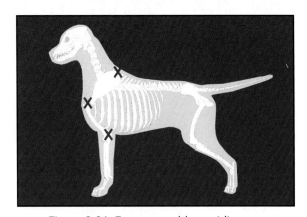

Figure 2-24: Front assembly equidistance

Front Assembly

Bones have to be balanced to work in unison. Equidistance means the dog will be able to move its front assembly muscles properly. With this in mind, most breeds should have the appearance of approximately the same length from the notch near the point of the shoulder to the top of the blade as from the notch to the elbow.

1. Shoulders. The shoulder blade should sit at the angle described in your breed standard, which, in most cases, is referred to as "well laid back" or "45 degrees."

Although there is an enormous amount of controversy regarding the feasibility of 45-degree shoulder angles on dogs, do not allow this controversy to become an excuse for not breeding the best you can. Remember, the straighter the shoulder, the shorter the reach.

The shoulder blades should fit smoothly and blend onto the rib cage. They should never be the highest point of the dog. In most breeds, you should not be able to see them, and you should hardly be able to feel them.

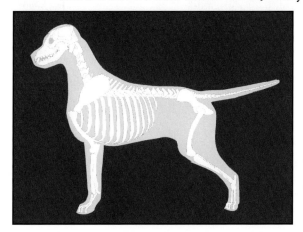
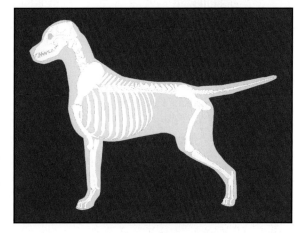

Figure 2-25: Good shoulders   Figure 2-26: High shoulders

If they "fit" properly, they will almost always have the proper space between the tips. If the tips are too far apart, the dog will move wide up front. If the tips are too close together, the dog's ability to lower its head will be restricted. And if a dog cannot eat out of a pan on the floor without laying down, how is it going to do the job for which it was originally bred, such as retrieve, hunt, or track?

2. Upper arm. Although you constantly hear in the show world about short upper arms, we see relatively few of them in our puppy evaluations. We see many more straight upper arms, with and without correct shoulders. Both straight and short upper arms can add to a soft topline.

3. Elbows. With your left hand over the puppy on its shoulder blades, push gently to the side. If this motion "pops" the elbow out, the dog will throw its elbows as an adult, which usually also causes the dog to toe in up front. This is the result of poor muscle attachment and/or loose ligaments.

4. Prosternum. The puppy should have a prosternum that you can almost hold onto with your fingers. Since a good prosternum surface is necessary for proper muscle attachment, which links the upper arm to the rib cage, a lack of prosternum may result in a very loose forward movement up front.

Depth of Chest

The depth of the chest at eight weeks should be what it is supposed to be as an adult. If the bottom of the chest is flat, the puppy will usually retain the depth. If it feels curved instead of flat, it will usually outgrow the depth you are feeling.

Also, put your hand on the chest between the front legs. If your fingers reach an angle under the ribs, the dog usually will have a herring gut. The depth of the ribs should extend to the ninth rib. If it does not, the resulting problem can affect the amount of stamina the dog has as an adult.

Figure 2-27: Good depth of chest

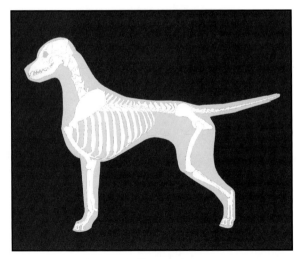

Figure 2-28: Herring gut

Length of Loin

The puppy's loin is measured from where the last rib comes off of the spine. The distance from the last rib to the pelvis should be shorter than the distance from the last rib to the shoulder.

If the puppy's loin is too long, the area between the last rib and the pelvis has no support. Therefore, the dog is going to be more susceptible to topline problems.

On the other hand, having too short of a loin is just as serious. All of the dog's ability to bend sideways resides in the loin. Some Terriers have gotten so short-backed that they don't have a loin left, so they are incapable of turning in or backing out of a hole. You have to get a shovel to dig them out after they get stuck.

Rear Assembly

As stated earlier, bones have to be balanced to work in unison. Equidistance means the dog will be able to move its rear assembly muscles properly.

Insofar as the rear assembly is concerned, the length between the point of the buttocks and the kneecap – or patella – should be approximately the same length as between the kneecap and the hock.

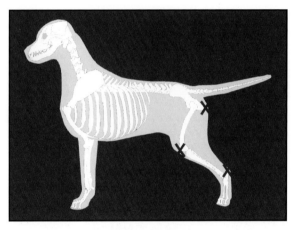

Figure 2-29: Rear assembly equidistance

1. Rear angulation. Breed standards vary enormously, when it comes to rear angulation. From the Chow Chow, expected to have a stifle with little angulation and an almost straight hock joint, to the Dachshund, expected to have right angles, and everything in between.

Just remember that at eight weeks, the stifle angle doesn't always show. It generally follows, however, that the sharper the hock angle, the more stifle angle the puppy will have as an adult. Just be sure you evaluate this piece in relation to your breed standard.

Rear assembly balance for most breeds is the same. Imagine dropping a plumb line down from the point of the buttocks to the ground. On a well-balanced, well-structured rear assembly, the plumb would drop right at the toes. This is the balance point required for proper movement.

If the rear legs are too long, and the feet fall far behind the plumb line, the puppy has **sickle hocks**. As it moves its feet forward for balance, the hocks appear to bend in the form of a sickle. This will affect the dog's movement, as it will have little or no range of motion behind.

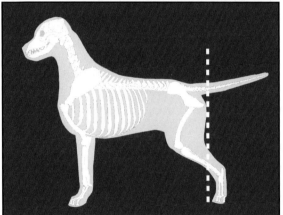 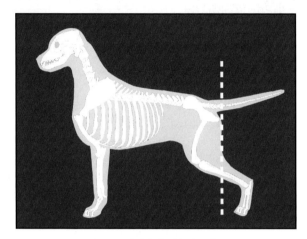

Figure 2-30: Proper rear assembly   Figure 2-31: Sickle hocks

2. Pelvis and musculature. All dogs from behind should be shaped like an inverted U. If the puppy you are evaluating is shaped like an inverted V, the puppy usually has a narrow pelvis and will move narrow behind.

If the puppy is a bitch, think carefully about whether you want to keep her in your breeding program, because a narrow pelvis increases the chance that you'll be paying for more caesarian sections, as well as potentially losing puppies due to prolonged deliveries and delays in electing to perform caesarian sections.

Generally speaking, the majority of breeds—with the notable exception of bulldogs—should never be narrower at the rear than they are at the shoulders.

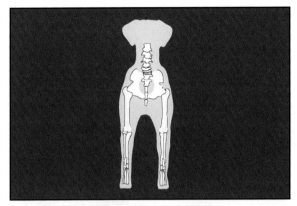

Figure 2-32: U-shaped pelvis

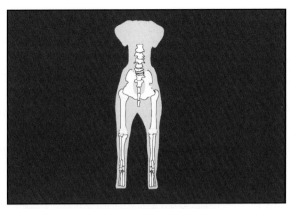

Figure 2-33: V-shaped pelvis

3. Knees. In most breeds, the kneecap—or patella—should flow into the body. If you evaluate a puppy whose knees point out, that puppy will be much more susceptible to injuries. Plus the abnormal weight bearing can result in added stress on the other joints in the rear assembly. Usually, a dog with knees angling out will move wide behind.

Luxating patellas—or slipped kneecaps—are not something we check for. You're much better off leaving that determination to your vet.

4. Placement of feet. When you're evaluating the rear, one of the things you look at is which way the rear feet point when you pick up the rear slightly and drop it. If the feet point out, the dog will stand and move as if it were cow-hocked, even if the dog is not cow-hocked.

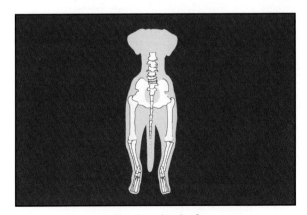

Figure 2-34: Cow hocks from rear

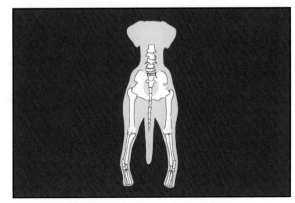

Figure 2-35: Open hocks from rear

Chapter 2 / TRICKS OF THE TRADE

A spread-, barrel-, or open-hocked dog will toe in behind with hocks out. Both this and cow hocks can be caused by an imbalance of muscle mass on the inside or outside of the leg. All muscles need to be balanced, in order to minimize the dog's susceptibility to injury.

5. Hocks. Hocks are the cornerstone of the rear assembly. The rear pastern should be perpendicular to the ground, and the hock joint itself should have no forward or side motion to it.

The shorter or more let down a hock is, the more endurance it will have. At eight weeks, the hock should be no more than one-third the total height of the dog's rear.

A potentially serious hock problem that is far too commonly seen is **slipped hocks**, also referred to as "double-jointed" or "popping" hocks. In the evaluation, the puppy with slipped hocks generally will not hold its rear in a stacked position. It will constantly be moving a rear leg forward.

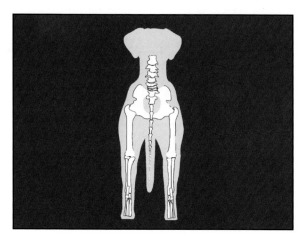

Figure 2-36: Good hocks from rear

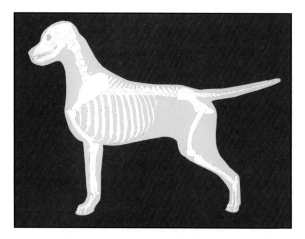

Figure 2-37: Good hocks from side

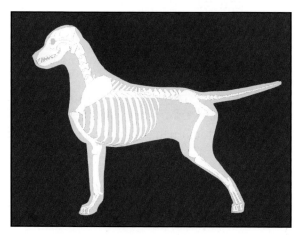

Figure 2-38: Slipped hocks from side

A slipped hock is when the joint itself bends the wrong direction—it hyperextends or collapses forward. The weakness is in the tissue, not the bone. The reason the puppy moves its leg or legs forward is because the hock joint will not collapse with the legs farther underneath the body. If a puppy has slipped hocks at eight weeks, it almost always has slipped hocks the rest of its life, no matter how it learns to compensate. But how many other problems does that compensation cause?

Hip dysplasia is thought to have a substantial genetic component. However, if a dog has a predisposition to hip problems and a joint beneath the hip wears out, the next joint up the line is going to take on more of the burden of balance and movement. When the hock wears out, the knee compensates. When the knee wears out, the hip compensates. Common sense tells us that all structures are composed of balance and compensation. Therefore, be aware that slipped hocks can cause the puppy serious problems later on, if the weakness is dismissed.

Topline

When you are looking at the topline of a puppy or dog, remember that where the bony projections on top of the vertebrae change direction, there is a slight dip. This is not a hole to be concerned about. A topline problem is very rarely created by the spine. It is usually a compensation issue. Therefore, to really understand the topline, we need to return to the front and rear assemblies.

1. Front assembly effect. If there is softness or there are holes in the topline, they usually stem from some problem in the front assembly. For example, if a puppy's front is too far forward, there will usually be a hole directly behind the shoulder blades. If a dog has straight shoulders or straight upper arms, it will usually have a soft topline. Wrinkles over the shoulders usually indicate straight or wide shoulder blades.

2. Rear assembly effect. If there is a roach to the topline—where there shouldn't be one—it usually stems from some problem in the rear assembly. Many dogs with slipped hocks will have roached toplines. In order to keep the pressure off their legs, they try to carry more weight in their backs. You can see the same effect in older dogs that have developed arthritis in their rear assemblies.

Croup and Tailset

If in your evaluation of a puppy you find that the croup and tailset are bad, you need to know that they'll probably never get better. If they're good, however, they can get worse over the next two years of the puppy's life.

The determining factors are the three vertebrae between the hip and the tailset. These vertebrae fuse together, and they are the last bones in the body to calcify.

The croup and tailset are dependent not only on the attitude of the dog but also on the rear structure. The weaker the structure is behind or the less chance a dog has to run in wide-open spaces, the greater your chances of losing a proper croup and tailset.

On an eight-week-old puppy, you want to see a tailset that's appropriate, with respect to your breed standard. With a tail that is supposed to be held up, you want to see a "shelf" or a protrusion of the buttocks behind the base of the tail. Exerting a slight forward pressure at the base of the tail should produce a 90-degree angle from the topline to the tailset.

With a tail that isn't suppose to be held up, you want the base of the tail to be a straight line down the rear. Also, at the intersection of the topline and the tail, you want a curve.

If the tailset or the rear is too high, check the point of the buttocks. This bone should feel like it's parallel with the ground. If it angles up, the puppy could have a tipped pelvis. In a bitch, this could contribute to whelping problems.

General Presentation

We do not evaluate movement in eight-week-old puppies. They are going to move however their brains tell them to, and brains aren't always in full communication with legs at eight weeks of age, especially in male puppies.

It's more important to watch puppies on the ground, because the way puppies use and carry their bodies—in other words, the way they naturally present themselves—generally stays with them throughout their lives.

The puppy on the ground who seems to say, "Just look at me: I'm fabulous," will almost always keep that kind of attitude. The one who walks around with its head tucked and shoulders slumped will usually grow up with that kind of attitude.

Also, the most difficult thing for any animal to do is to stand still. The same is true for people. In order for a dog to be comfortable standing still, it has to be well made and balanced. So the puppy that stands proud, without fidgeting, is probably the most well-structured puppy in the litter.

The more structurally imbalanced a puppy is, the more it's in motion. Additionally, the best-built puppies usually trot. The ones that bunny-hop usually have the greater number of structural weaknesses.

Substance

The size and substance of an eight-week-old puppy mean very little. The smallest puppy in the litter can turn out to be the biggest dog, and vice versa. However, a puppy should weigh what you think it's going to weigh. In other words, when picking a puppy up, you shouldn't be surprised by the weight in your hands.

This has to do with bone density, and if bone density is out of balance with the rest of the puppy, it can grow up either spindly or clunky. Remember, physical structure is all about compensation and balance.

CONCLUSION

The three most important reasons to evaluate litters of puppies you have bred are:

1. To determine whether there are structural problems. If there's a structural problem, search out the cause. You can't fix anything in a breeding program until you know specifically what needs to be fixed. It doesn't do any good to look at a dog and say: "I don't like that rear," unless you know why you don't like it and what is needed to improve it.

2. To determine which puppies to keep in your breeding program. Use all elements of the formula for success. In other words, consider the results of your structural evaluations in conjunction with breed type, coat, colors, and preferences.

3. To determine what kind of home is most suitable for each puppy that leaves you. It is up to you, as the breeder, to make a match between a prospective buyer's lifestyle and the puppy whose structural qualities are most compatible.

There is no substitute for careful, responsible breeding. The only thing more important is to put the welfare of the puppies you breed before all else when making your decisions about where and how they will spend the rest of their lives.

Objective evaluations and careful record keeping can advance your breeding program, your breed, and possibly your show wins. But of course, there is more to winning than simply producing or buying a great puppy. Always remember: Whole package, whole package, whole package!

Success is a journey, not a destination.

nutrition

FOOD FOR GROWING PUPPIES

When you consider that a puppy grows for 18 to 20 months and a child grows for 18 to 20 years, the speed at which damage can be done by improper puppy nutrition is staggering. Feeding a puppy improperly for one month is the equivalent of feeding a child improperly for one year. Thus, it is imperative to make sure your puppies are doing well on whatever you are feeding them. Just remember how quickly nutritional damage can occur, and once the growth plates close, nutritional damage is permanent.

One issue we as consumers must give careful thought to is the idea that more is better. Why would we want to feed our puppies more powerful nutrients than we feed our adult dogs? The overwhelming consumer response would be: "Because they're growing babies."

Let's think about that one for a moment. Do human babies receive more powerful nutrients than human adults? They start out on formula or breast milk, then slowly move to strained, bland fruits and vegetables. They are hardly coaxed to gum down salads, steaks, or multigrain dinner rolls. When was the last time you saw an infant chomp into a pepperoni pizza?

By the same token, do coyote pups or wolf cubs get the prime morsels of their parents' hunt? Certainly not. They either receive a regurgitated portion of the kill or morsels left over after the adults have eaten.

In a sense, we as consumers may have convinced the dog food companies that we want special food for our growing puppies and that we are willing to pay extra for it. And no one in Corporate America's right mind would ignore that kind of message. So it goes—we give the message that more is better, and we believe if something on the market costs more, it must be better. But what does this cycle mean for our puppies?

High-powered nutrients can make it possible to grow bone faster than it is meant to grow. However, the growth rate of tissue is unalterable. If a puppy receives more nutrients than it can utilize so that those nutrients accelerate the growth rate of bones beyond the growth rate of tissue, the tissue can be weakened.

When we conduct our puppy evaluations, we always pay close attention to how puppies are doing on the food they're being given. When we see nutritionally-based problems, our first recommendation is always to drop back one level in the quality of food the puppies are eating. This change almost always corrects the nutritional problems we see in front legs and feet. (See Chapter 2, Puppy Evaluations.)

Try to feed puppies only what their systems and structures can use. If your puppies are running in the woods with their mother from five or six weeks on, they are spending enough energy to utilize almost any level of nutrients you choose to feed them. However, most of us raise our puppies in small yards, kennels, exercise pens, and kitchens. In these cases, we need to be careful about what we feed.

Also, smaller breeds burn greater amounts of energy in confined spaces, so less damage is seen when these puppies are fed more high-powered nutrients. By the same token, however, the smaller the breed, the smaller the space provided, so nutritional damage is possible.

We recommend you feed a name-brand product that clearly states it is formulated for all stages of a dog's life. If you see any structural weaknesses that could be caused by what is being fed, switching to a lesser-power food generally corrects the problem, as long as the growth plates have not yet closed. The younger the puppy is when this change is made, the faster the problem is corrected. As stated earlier, the nutritionally-based weakness becomes permanent once the growth plates have closed.

We believe if you are feeding a quality food to your adult dogs and they are in excellent condition, then that is what you should be feeding your puppies from day one.

Puppies should be given only their food. Try not to offset the balance of this nutritional formula by adding other food items or supplements. The only supplement we suggest is Vitamin C. A study out of Cornell University indicates that a Vitamin C supplement allows a dog to utilize more readily the available calcium in their bodies. Giving dogs a calcium supplement can cause more problems than it cures.

Supplementing with Vitamin C, which is water-soluble, can help only if help is needed. Vitamin C is part of the enzyme that links and strengthens collagen—a vital component of tendons, ligaments, and joints. So even though Vitamin C supplementation may be controversial in some circles, its use poses little potential for harm.

DOG FOODS AND FEEDING

Buyer beware: Reading labels can be a waste of time. The ingredients listed on dog food packages may be what's in the food, but there is no way to know what the quality of those ingredients is or what percentage may be available for appropriate utilization.

Best rule of thumb: If what you're feeding works, don't let anyone talk you out of it. If it isn't working, try another food. Continuing with a food that isn't working well for your dogs then adding to it only means you are spending more money and effort than is necessary. There are many good-quality foods and diets available. Use what works for your dogs.

In keeping with this philosophy, have you ever wondered why 15 or so dog food companies all claim to have "proof" that their products are the best? Remember marketing does not a miracle dog food make. Stick to what's right for you and your dogs.

There are, however, four proven facts with regard to feeding:

- ❖ Dogs stay in better condition if they are fed more than once a day.
- ❖ Dogs are better eaters if they eat warm food.
- ❖ Dogs are better eaters if they have more than one texture to their food.
- ❖ Most owners overfeed their dogs.

One more note: Be careful with supplementation. If dogs are missing something they need, a supplement can help. If your dogs are in good condition, a supplement can destroy that condition. As with puppies, give your

Chapter 3 / TRICKS OF THE TRADE

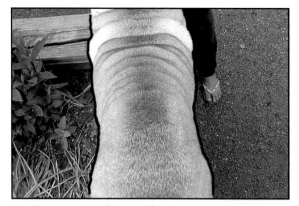

Figure 3-01: Chinese Shar-Pei in good weight

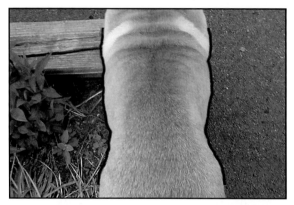

Figure 3-02: Chinese Shar-Pei underweight

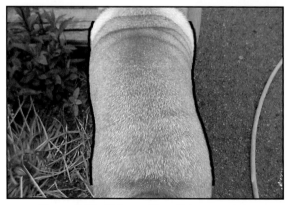

Figure 3-03: Chinese Shar-Pei overweight

dogs only what they need. As soon as you have fixed a problem, stop using whatever you used to fix it. And never use a supplement just because someone else does.

A HEALTHY WEIGHT

As far as weight condition, there are three elements to check for on your dog:

1. You should be able to feel all of the ribs with your hand, but your fingers should not fall between them.

2. You should be able to find the hip bones easily by touch, but they should not be visible (unless your breed standard calls for it).

3. When looking straight down on the topline of most breeds of dog, you should be able to see an indication of a waist.

An excellent habit to get into is to regularly look at your dogs before you feed them. If they're getting thin, feed them more. If they are getting fat, feed them less. Monitoring their weight day by day is so much easier than working to fix a weight problem once it has become all too obvious.

According to Dr. Janet Cook, from a study done at UC Davis, "lite" foods do not satisfy the daily requirements for a healthy, active animal. Therefore, they should only be regularly fed to dangerously overweight dogs. For dogs simply on the hefty side, a lite food may not be the best approach to dieting.

We have found that the best way for us to take weight off of a dog is to feed it exactly what we have been feeding it all of its life and in the same bowl it has eaten from all its life. We just cut the food ration in half and make up the difference in volume with unsalted, unbuttered popcorn or rice cakes. This fills the dog's stomach without changing its regular food. Most dogs will lose weight rapidly on this regimen.

To put weight on a dog, first try feeding a lesser formula of the brand of food you feed. Sometimes, cutting down available nutrients makes it easier for them to utilize all of the food, and they can actually gain weight.

Second, try Lactinex, an inexpensive, live stomach enzyme product. It can be purchased at pharmacies and must be refrigerated. Add one tablet per 50 pounds of the dog's weight to the dog's food. Don't use more than one bottle. If Lactinex is going to work, one bottle's worth will get the stomach back on track. If there is relatively no change in the dog's weight after one bottle, it's not going to work, so stop using it. After all, there is no sense in using something that is ineffective.

Third, try the high-nutrition, high-calorie human drinks such as Ensure. Just add some to the food. It adds calories without adding volume. This matters because adding volume can cause loose stools, which in turn can cause the dog to lose additional weight.

Put an underweight dog on a good multi-vitamin, as any deficiency in zinc and B vitamins can cause an impaired sense of smell and taste, which can contribute to weight loss.

Excessive weight on a dog is the more dangerous of the two conditions. An underweight dog may never have a great coat, since ingested nutrients are busy maintaining necessary body functions first, so there may be little left over to grow hair. But when a dog is overweight, its structure is compromised, especially if that structure is already less than sound and balanced. Discomfort from slipped hocks, hip dysplasia, or arthritis is aggravated by excessive weight. The dog's lungs, heart, and circulatory system must work harder than they are meant to if the dog is obese.

We have all been faced with a dog's pathetically pleading countenance when we pull out a snack for ourselves. If the guilt is too much, remember that raw baby carrots make an excellent diet treat for dogs. They are crunchy, contain no calories, and get you off the hook.

*Someone who thinks logically provides
a nice contrast to the real world.*

teaching a dog to learn

Dogs are not born with the instinctual ability to learn from humans. Learning is a taught behavior. So the more words we teach our dogs, the larger their vocabulary becomes, and the more capable they are of learning. That is the first rule of thumb. The second rule of thumb is never do something for a dog that you can teach it to do for itself. Much like human children, puppies grow up more confident when they are taught to think for themselves. If you do for dogs, they will rely on you instead of using their own brains.

INTERACTING WITH PUPPIES

The most important qualities you can instill in your puppies are self-confidence and an awareness of appropriate boundaries.

❖ **Teach instead of train.** Puppies are much like our own children; they will match their cunning against ours. Psychology is at work—it is wise not to underestimate this aspect in puppies or adult dogs. In order to teach puppies, we must think through each situation and pay attention to our behavior as well as theirs.

❖ **Never overdo anything with a puppy.** The second a puppy tells you "that's enough," believe it—that's enough. The most important thing to remember about your puppies is to let them be puppies.

❖ **Imprinting a pattern of behavior is one of the easiest ways to teach.** For example, when you start walking puppies and they're learning what the world is all about, as well as the vocabulary that goes along with it, save one toy that can only be played with during a walk. You can make a game out of them carrying this toy in their mouths on walks. They will learn to keep their heads up when they are on lead because of the toy they carry. And forming this type of habit, which is a behavior pattern, will last a lifetime.

❖ **Every time you pick up a puppy for any reason—be it one from a litter of yours or a puppy you have purchased—put it on a grooming table.** The grooming table is all important because it is the most valuable conditioning and teaching tool you have.

Make sure your table is in a convenient place, and have it in front of a mirror, so you learn to look at the dog in the mirror, as opposed to looking directly at the dog. Each time you put the dog on a table, put it in a show stance. This is something a dog learns by doing—another case of imprinting a behavior pattern. And while you're at it, imprint a behavior pattern on yourself: Always look at the dog while you position it or do anything with it, THEN look in the mirror to see the results. This is important to learn, because if you look in the mirror while you are doing something, you'll only confuse yourself.

As for the dog, just stack it on the table, without fanfare or instruction. Avoid setting up a "push comes to shove" interaction with the dog. For example, in order to avoid creating a counterforce from the dog when you're moving a leg, shift the weight off of the leg before moving it. This is a sensible concept to remember: All dogs oppose force, so avoid teaching your dogs to resist what you do. Start from the beginning of your puppies' lives to form the habit of "teaching" instead of "training."

Every time you do anything to that puppy—look at it, do its nails, check its mouth, clean its ears, weigh it, whatever—put it on the table in a show stance, keeping the head in a stacked position, moving legs in the same fashion you would in a show ring. In this way, you are imprinting on the puppy's mind what you expect of it.

The more you place a puppy on a table in this manner, the more it will stand in a show position. Do all of this in a teaching, instead of a training, fashion in order to continually set the puppy up for success rather than failure.

WORKING WITH DOGS

In order to have the best dogs, form a lifelong mind-set of teaching dogs instead of training them. This is a positive approach, both for the dog and for you, since teaching is a process of providing guidance toward appropriate behavior.

For example, when a dog acts tense or spooky, ignore it. By making an issue of a dog's negative behavior, you may inadvertently encourage that behavior. To develop good behavior in a dog, ignore the dog when it behaves badly (within reason) and reward it when it behaves well. That way, the dog learns for itself how to behave. Use common sense, however, as there are some behaviors that must never be ignored, such as biting. All dogs must learn that biting is completely unacceptable (schutzhund competition aside).

By the same token, if you focus on a problem, it may become a more entrenched problem. Find a way around the difficulty. This is a greater challenge for you than for the dog. An example would be a dog that shies when a judge is going over it. Perhaps the worst treatment for this problem is to make the dog endure people going over it in numerous practice runs for the show ring. Instead, take the dog to agility classes, so it will focus on the fun of the activity rather than the people who are coming up to pet it.

❖ **The first rule of teaching is to help the dog understand you are the teacher.** This is accomplished with your voice, you body language, and your control over all situations. All dogs need a pack leader–they need to know someone is in control. If you are not that someone, then the dog will take the position upon itself, whether it wants the job or not.

This can create an intolerable situation–the dog may grow to be uncontrollable, vicious, neurotic, or so confused and uneasy as to make itself ill. Successful teaching begins with your resolve and your confidence. Dogs will learn from those in whom they can believe and take seriously.

For physical control, if you have control of a dog's head, you have control of the dog. This is imperative when teaching dogs, because if dogs think they can win, they will continue to fight you. If they know they cannot win, they stop fighting and settle down. And only when dogs are calm can they concentrate on learning.

There is no winning arguments with dogs, so don't argue with them. If they know you are in charge, they will accept and respect your authority. Therefore, be willing to be the teacher; be the pack leader. It may require "tough love," but it is well worth the effort.

❖ **Help the dog build confidence by finding ways to teach it to think and do for itself.** For example, if the dog sidewinds in the ring, it may simply be resisting tension on its lead. Change the position of the collar, then walk the dog without tension on the lead and see what happens. All dogs need to believe they have a say in their lives. In order for a show dog to have a long career, they have to believe it was part their idea to want to be a show dog. Therefore, in order to prepare a dog to be a show dog, you have to be smarter than they are, or at least convince them that you are smarter. This can be a tricky proposition at times. The very best way to teach is to exercise your own best measure of common sense.

❖ **The reason a dog responds to a professional handler without a lot of pre-show practice is that good professional handlers know how to communicate what they want from the dogs.** Whenever you can make dogs think that changing their behavior is their idea, you are helping them present themselves as better show dogs. When a dog looks like it is showing itself, you are communicating well with your dog.

You cannot make dogs do things they don't want to do and expect them to look happy about it. You want to make being a show dog something they want to be. The more you practice with a dog, the more bored it becomes, hence the less of a show dog it is.

However, if you work your dogs on a grooming table, they never seem to relate it to what's asked of them on the ground. First, you're not putting dogs in a submissive position when working them on a table. The more you work over the top of a dog on the floor, the more the dog gets the message that you want him or her to be submissive, and submissive dogs are less than great show dogs. Dogs must be taught how to stack and show like a show dog–they can't be forced into playing the part.

❖ **When it comes to lead work, we believe in lead-teaching, as opposed to lead-breaking, a show dog.** Dogs are best lead-taught on a buckle collar and a retractable or long lead. The reason for this is that the average dog owner has a tendency to jerk or pull on a short leash or show lead. A retractable or long lead teaches the person to talk more and yank less.

With puppies on lead, never make them go anywhere they don't want to go. Instead, carry them to where they don't want to be, then let them walk back.

All of the time the dogs or puppies are walking on lead, talk to them. Discuss things they're interested in–the fire hydrant or the flower beds you're passing. (Face it; your neighbors probably already think you're nuts, so it does no harm to add some fuel to the fire.) Talk to them constantly and positively. In this way, you are conditioning them to respond to your voice.

❖ **If you have a dog that paces (moves both legs on the same side in the same direction), the easiest way to convince it that pacing doesn't pay is to find a hill on which to walk the dog.** Walk the dog along the side of the hill so that if it paces, it falls over. Two or three falls usually will convince the dog to gait correctly. If your dog spends part of its day in a kennel or run, placing PCV pipe (or something similar) through the wire in such a way that the dog has to step over it, but cannot jump over it, will help break the habit of pacing. A dog is unable to pace and step over something at the same time.

❖ **When it comes to baiting, we generally had greater success teaching dogs to bait off-lead.** The dog is only given bait when it has done something for it; this way, it learns bait is something to be earned, unlike food or treats. Use only a bait that the dog wants; otherwise, you'll find you

Chapter 4 / TRICKS OF THE TRADE

are teaching the dog to refuse things. Remember to practice only what brings about the results desired.

When baiting in the ring, use a large piece of bait that the dog can see, but never gait the dog with bait in your hand. Put the bait in your pocket, show the dog that it is no longer in your hand, then off you go. When the dog has done what you have asked of it, bait immediately, using only a tidbit from a large piece. Bait is meant to be a reward, not a meal.

Throughout the teaching process, use a tidbit of bait to reinforce the dog's positive response to every command—everytime. After appropriate behavior has been established, switch to a variable reinforcement approach; that is, the dog gets a reward of bait part of the time, but continues to receive praise all of the time. If the dog's behavior backslides at any point, return to constant rewards until the behavior is back on track.

❖ **The easiest way to start teaching dogs to do certain things is to teach them the words for what they're going to do.** If you know your dog is going to sit when you come up with a treat, teach it the word "sit" before it sits. If you know your dog is going to wag its tail when it sees something in particular, teach it to wag its tail. Use every opportunity to teach.

❖ **Handling classes may be one of the worst things you can do for a show prospect.** Handling classes are unbelievably important for handlers, but do your learning at such classes with a pet or a retired show dog, any canine but your show prospects. Show dogs can get incredibly bored at handling classes, and bored dogs make poor show dogs. Although dogs learn by repetition, the more you repeat something, the more dogs lose interest. Going through the motions of being a show dog for an hour at a time in class can easily destroy a show attitude. And attitude is part of the whole package. You need to learn how to handle a dog so it knows what you want of it in the show ring—that is the best use of handling classes. Until you learn how to teach and communicate with your dogs, practice with a pet. Once you learn what you need to know, then you can become the teacher.

Dogs need socialization time, and handling classes can meet that need. However, if you take your show prospects to handling classes for socialization purposes, take them on equipment that is not used for show. If you take them on show equipment, you're going to go through the motions of making them look and act like a show dog. If you take them on a buckle collar and retractable or long lead, you'll avoid that temptation. This way, the dogs can get used to the situation on their terms instead of on your terms. Remember, they are there for socialization; you are there to learn.

Furthermore, you are responsible for your dog in any social setting, so pay close attention to interactions and reactions, and be on the lookout for canine rudeness (unacceptably crossing another dog's personal boundaries). Otherwise, retractable or long leads can get you and your dog into trouble.

❖ **If you have a dog that is shy or backs off or crouches in strange situations, always try to put that dog in a position to succeed.** Asking a dog to do something it is not yet capable of dealing with is inviting failure. Instead, try to figure out a way around the problem.

For example, take a table to the handling class and put the dog on the table, where no one will be doing anything to frighten it or make it submissive. Let the dog decide that this situation is okay. (Make sure you pay the required class fee for this opportunity.) Use your grooming arm, and stay with the dog to make sure nothing happens; at the same time, don't protect it or do its thinking for it. Dogs need to learn they are responsible for themselves. The dog should remain on the table until it has made the decision that all is well. It can then be worked on the ground. One dog may get comfortable with the situation in one class; another dog may take weeks of classes to come to the same conclusion. Each dog will take as long as it needs, so be patient.

❖ **Dogs dislike and respond negatively to being nagged (much like spouses and kids do).** And, although we may not want to admit it, we know nagging is ultimately self-defeating. With this admission, do everything in your power to break this habit. Try to avoid using the word "no." It is very possibly the first word that both dogs and kids learn to ignore or tune out. Moreover, saying "no" robs the dog of initiative, as well as a willingness to keep trying.

Chapter 4 / TRICKS OF THE TRADE

❖ **According to many experts, almost everything that happens in people happens in dogs.** Most people think a dog is just a dog and you can do anything with or to them, but that is not true. They are all individuals. Dogs are right- or left-handed. Dogs can be slow or fast learners. There is mental retardation and insanity in some dogs. Some dogs are heterosexual; some dogs are homosexual. (This point, of course, begs the question of how can sexual preference be a conscious choice if some animals are gay?) Dogs can be far-sighted or near-sighted. A dog with depth-perception problems, for instance, can be uncomfortable on a table because of its height.

There is Downs Syndrome in dogs, and it looks very much as it does in humans. There is hyperactivity in dogs, and vets sometimes use Ritalin to help alleviate symptoms. There is depression, and vets use Prozac. There is attention deficit disorder, as well as Alzheimer's.

Dogs face as broad of a range of mental, emotional, and physical challenges as we do. So you have to learn how to read dogs well enough to understand and accept that all dogs are not fixable, they're not all doable. All living things have a stress threshold that cannot be crossed. Try never to push beyond that point in your dogs. Sometimes, you have to cut your losses and move on.

❖ **The expression "it's okay" is one of the worst things you can say to a dog when it is behaving contrary to what you expect or need.** It is also one of the most difficult expressions to eliminate from your response file. Dogs cannot reason as people do; they cannot understand you are referring to the situation. They think they're being praised for their behavior.

For example, a dog fussing on the table hears "it's okay" and thinks it's okay to be fussy or in constant motion on the table. Generally, the most successful way to break the habit of saying "it's okay" is to work the dog with someone else around who can help you break the habit.

Find a replacement expression, such as "you can do this" or "you can be brave," and use it often. After awhile, your mind will reach for it before you have a chance to say "it's okay."

❖ **Once more with feeling: Don't do anything for a dog that you can teach the dog to do for itself.** A good example is placing a dog on a table. If you pick it up and put it on the table, you're depriving yourself and your dog of an opportunity to learn. The small breeds are picked up and set on the table. However, with larger breeds, teach the dogs to put their front feet on the end of the table, then you boost the rear and teach them to walk forward on the table while you are boosting.

Besides what this approach teaches, it has two advantages. First, it is less stressful for your body to support a dog getting on a table versus picking it up. Second, it is inadvisable to teach dogs to jump onto tables. Tables with a high center of gravity can tip if a large dog comes zooming up onto it from a bad angle. If your table is on a slick or unlevel surface, accidents can happen. Also, a dog allowed to jump up on a table can cause problems in the show ring. Imagine how mortified you might be if you are running your dog around the ring and as you go by a table, the dog jumps on the table instead of continuing around the ring—it does happen.

The same thing applies to taking a dog off of the table. Let a dog leave a table only when you want it to get off. Support the dog underneath its loins with one hand and hold the collar or lead in your other hand, then teach the dog to get off.

Dogs are intelligent, intuitive, emotional beings. To treat them as any less is a disservice to the dogs with which we live, work, and compete. Moreover, discounting a dog's cognitive capabilities short-changes our own. Let's face it, teaching is a challenge to our wits and creativity—rewarding for both the person who accepts that challenge and the dog.

Chapter 4 / TRICKS OF THE TRADE

Every person you meet knows something you don't; learn from them.

dog wherewithal

We all started in the sport of purebred dogs because we love dogs. However, sometimes we lose sight of that. It is particularly important, then, to take a moment every so often to remember that the dog is what's most important—the dog should have priority.

If you are spending so much time taking care of your dogs that you have no time to enjoy them, then maybe you have too many dogs. It is a different number of dogs for every single person, but for the sake (and well-being) of your animals, find out what your limit is and stay within it.

Moreover, I firmly believe that every dog we own should be, in a manner of speaking, for sale. If someone comes along who can give one of my dogs a happier life and a home better suited to that particular dog, then the dog should have the right to go with that person, to that home.

With all that dogs offer us in their relatively short lifetimes, don't they deserve the best we can offer them?

PUPPIES AND LITTERS

❖ **Whether you are breeding or buying, avoid keeping littermates, if possible.** Littermates have a tendency to bond with each other, like twins. A dog that forms strong bonds with a littermate may not form strong bonds with humans. Another risk with littermates is that they may hate each other as they mature.

Still another risk is that one littermate will be overly dominant, which may ruin the more submissive sibling. Is it worth the gamble that the best dog you ever bred or owned in your life ends up being an inadequate show dog because of one of these situations?

❖ **The changes puppies go through while they are growing up can drive you nuts if you keep looking at them.** One week, they will look great; the next week, they may look horrible; the next week, great again; the next week, so average as to be nondescript.

Make your decisions about puppies when they are eight weeks old, or at the age you deem appropriate, then put all decision-making on hold until the dogs are mature, which can be varying ages, depending on breed and bloodlines.

Too many breeders lean toward making decisions when the puppies look the way the breeders want them to look, which is oftentimes an unsuccessful approach. Remember, growing puppies can go into a good stage, then into a bad stage, and on and on, until they are structurally mature.

At the same time, it is unfair to our dogs to "grow out" litters and make our decisions when the puppies are older. I believe every puppy deserves its own home to grow up in and its own family with whom to bond. By the time puppies are 4, 6, 9, or 12 months old, they have left behind a developmental stage that is better experienced in its permanent home.

❖ **Color-marking puppies in each litter is an excellent idea.** However, be careful what you use. We always color-marked with the strips of material used to make potholders. These strips are called loom loopers and are readily available at most toy or hobby stores. They're inexpensive and elastic, so if they catch on something, the puppy can get free easily. Bear in mind, however, that Murphy's Law might as well have been designed to apply to breeding dogs: If something bad can happen, it will. Best to keep a close eye on your puppies, whatever material you decide to use.

In addition to being able to identify every puppy from birth, another reason to color-code puppies is to avoid giving them nicknames. If you call them "pink" and "blue" and "green," they usually don't end up with permanent names like "Tiny Tim" and "Big Bertha." You can be more objective about puppies if they don't have names; they are easier to part with and easier to evaluate. After all, how many of us have used a favorite name on a pup that didn't make the grade? I christened a puppy at birth with one of my favorite names; when I lost that puppy at 10 days old, I was too superstitious to ever again bestow that name on another puppy.

If you are going to color-code puppies, do it at birth so that the mother thinks the "collar" is just part of the puppy. It is also beneficial when the time comes for puppies to wear real collars and begin lead work.

RAISING PUPPIES

❖ **When supplementing is required, bottle feeding is preferred over tubing.** The release of enzymes that enhance digestion is stimulated by suckling, and tube-feeding does not involve suckling.

❖ **It is imperative to keep a substantial supply of safe toys around for your puppies and to introduce them to toys when they are infants.** Toys—of varied weights and textures—that roll, squeak, and smell interesting will draw their attention as soon as they have their tactile senses.

Early introduction and rotation of toys imprints on the puppies what items are appropriate for wrestling and chewing. Without this imprinting activity, puppies are more likely to be nondiscriminating in their destructive play.

A wonderful way for you to interact with your puppies is with a kid's favorite—soap bubbles. Puppies love them, and you can monitor the development of their coordination, temperament, and personality, as well as their position in the pecking order of the litter.

Another great toy is a good-quality car wash mitt, because puppies do not seem to be as capable of destroying it nearly as well as they destroy actual dog toys made of the same type of material. A word of caution, however: the cuff on a car wash mitt can be chewed to bits with very little effort. It's advisable to remove the cuff before tossing the mitt to enthusiastic puppies.

❖ **Environmental challenges at an early age aid in the development of the nervous system which controls coordination.** The challenges need not be elaborate. Things to climb over, crawl under, and go through can be enough. Crates taken apart and put on the ground with the solid part up can serve as both a den and a high place.

Kids' toys, such as Little Tykes® pre-school play pieces, hanging tires, concrete drainage pipes, steel drums, and large PCV pipes can all help build confidence as well as coordination. Beginning pieces of agility equipment are fabulous.

STRUCTURAL REVIEW

One of the most significant pearls of wisdom I was fortunate to receive over the years was in these words: A sound dog will age more gracefully, be less likely to break down from stress or injury, experience less fatigue and greater efficiency in work, and stay healthier and more attractive throughout its life.

Sound structure is as imperative for obedience and working dogs as it is for show dogs—sometimes, even more so. For example, the more you exercise a dog with wide shoulders, the worse those shoulders will become. If a dog's shoulders are not formed around the ribcage, they tend to muscle under the blade. If the shoulders fit tight, the muscles form over the shoulder.

Another example is in the whole of a dog's front assembly. If the front assembly is unsound, the dog could break down from jumping. And it isn't the amount of jumping done in the obedience or agility ring that wears the structure out; it is the hundreds of practice jumps the dog does getting ready for competition.

Sixty percent of a dog's weight is carried in the front half of its body. When dogs jump, they push off with their rear legs and land on their front legs. Therefore, every time a dog lands on an unsound front assembly, the tissues give and stretch until finally they wear out.

A well-trained dog will go beyond its physical limitations to do what we ask until it has nothing left to give, and it is grossly unfair of us to ask more of a dog than it is physically structured to give.

And what happens when dogs reach the point of breakdown? The average owner's initial tendency is to get frustrated with the dog. More times than I can count, my husband and I have been approached by someone wanting to know why their dog suddenly won't take the jumps after so many good obedience performances. These people want to know why their dogs are suddenly being disobedient or just plain lazy.

In almost every case we have encountered, the dog's structure has broken down. Most people are genuinely unaware of their dogs' physical condition when such behavior patterns begin to emerge. The body is simply telling the dog it cannot do another jump. How long before the dog reaches this point of breakdown depends largely on the owner's awareness of and respect for the dog's inherent physical strengths and weaknesses.

A dog or bitch with unsound structure needs to be spayed or neutered and placed in a home that will ask of it only what it can handle. Some poorly structured dogs are best suited to be placed in homes where they can be free to be couch potatoes. Some just need homes where the most that is expected of them is to run and play with the kids.

When evaluating your dog for show, remember that evaluating adult dogs is entirely different than evaluating puppies. With puppies, you look for anything that could be a structural challenge or problem to ensure the puppy is placed in the best kind of home or lifestyle for that puppy's physical capabilities. With an adult dog, you always want to look at its virtues first.

A valuable habit to form is to find and verbalize five desirable qualities in any dog before you say one bad thing about it. Then when you look at the faults, you will be more likely to put them in perspective—weigh them against the qualities you verbalized. Do the qualities outweigh the faults?

Try this at ringside, even with your most formidable competitor's dog. Never say anything bad about a dog, not even to yourself, until you have said five good things about it. Not only will it make you a better dog person, but you may find the approach to be contagious.

Be warned: One of the worst faults is to imagine your dog has no faults. Like all other living things, no dog is perfect. Convincing yourself that your dog is perfect is one of the worst mistakes you can make. After all, you can make no improvements if you are unwilling to see or unable to understand what needs to be improved. Deluding yourself into thinking your dog is flawless could diminish on your credibility in the dog world.

Chapter 5 / TRICKS OF THE TRADE

Do everything in your power to learn all you can about both canine structure and breed standards. All too often, people tend to learn only what is within their immediate interest, so their knowledge remains limited. You can't blame people for not knowing what they don't know. However, greater respect is earned by those who live their lives as students. To the best of your ability, always broaden your horizons beyond your immediate boundaries.

Structure is to a great extent mandated by genetics. However, some structural problems rest squarely on our shoulders. For instance, a dog's feet can be destroyed by long toenails. Tendons and ligaments do not contain the type of cells that allow for retraction if these tissues have been overextended or hyperextended. When a dog's nails touch the ground, nature provides a way out, if we do not. The foot will begin to roll in order to compensate. As the foot rolls, the tendons and ligaments begin to stretch. No dog deserves to lose the full capability of its feet, but a show dog is in part judged by what the breed standard says about the foot. Regular nail care is all it takes.

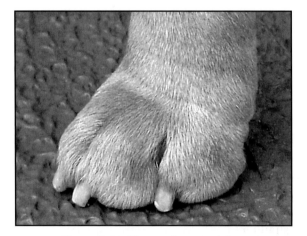

Figure 5-01: Short nails, sound foot

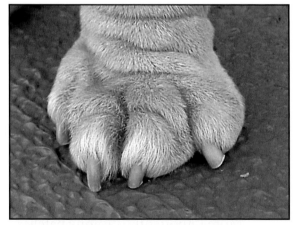

Figure 5-02: Foot damaged by long nails

Slipped hocks are a very common structural fault that can physically impair the dog. Placed in a pet home, a dog with slipped hocks will probably have few difficulties. But dogs will do whatever we ask them to do, even if we are asking more than their bodies are capable of handling over an extended period of time. Despite structural weaknesses, dogs will do obedience work and herding, lure coursing and agility, until they are no longer able to physically meet these challenges. Is that fair to do to the dogs we profess to love?

With slipped hocks, sporting dogs can become worthless in the field because there is no stability on rough ground. Swimming dogs may take a dislike to water, because a dog needs stability in its rear legs in order to swim. If the hock is flopping around, the dog probably will high-tail it out of the water and tell you to go get the duck yourself. Herding dogs and coursing dogs generally lose the ability to make fast corners safely.

Once the tissue in a joint wears out, chances are it will develop arthritis as the dog ages.

This point leads us to the subject of patella (knee) problems. This is a totally different problem from hocks, since slipped hocks stem from a tissue problem, while slipped or luxating patellas usually stem from a bone problem.

One of the most common genetic reasons for luxating patellas is that the groove in which the kneecap (ie, patella) sits is too shallow. It is best to have your vet check the dog's knees instead of checking them yourself, because it's very easy to hurt the dog in the process unless you know exactly what to do. However, have the knees checked only after the dog is eight weeks old, since it takes the first eight weeks for tissue to develop its natural strength. A dog frequently seen skipping or stretching a rear leg back for no apparent reason is giving evidence of a need to visit the vet.

Slipped or luxating patellas worked beyond their capacity or left untended can cause tremendous damage and pain. Being aware of this problem early on can save the dog a great deal of discomfort. However, bear in mind that a surgical correction makes the dog ineligible for the show ring. More importantly, luxating patellas are usually genetic, so although you may show a dog with bad knees, it would be an extremely bad idea to include that dog in a breeding program.

If you need more reasons to expand your working knowledge of canine structure, I offer these: A dog acquired for jumping in obedience or agility should have no looseness in the elbows or lack in prosternum, both of which can cause stretched and damaged tissue in the front assembly. A sporting dog with a ewe neck or a weak underjaw may eventually be incapable of carrying a bird. A ewe neck in a water breed may even make for a poor swimmer.

Figure 5-03: Afghan Hound—Lure Coursing

Figure 5-04: German Shepard Dog—Obedience

Figure 5-05: Chesapeake Bay Retriever—Field Trial

Figure 5-06: Siberian Huskies—Sledding

A dog bred to go to ground is fairly useless if its loin is too short or nonexistent. A herring gut or high hocks diminish stamina. An overangulated rear, which creates sickle hocks, causes a poorly synchronized gait, which destroys efficiency of movement. High shoulders are one of the most destructive weaknesses that a dog in harness can have. Shoulders set too close together can impede the ability of a tracking dog to keep its nose to the ground. Too low of a tailset interferes with an effortless gait. Too high of a tailset can prevent a dog from being capable of pulling a cart.

We owe our dogs the effort of developing a good eye and sensitive hand to structural weaknesses. Perfection may be unattainable, but the striving yields its own rewards—and that striving must include learning all we can.

CARING FOR THE SHOW DOG

The reason top handlers (and I am talking about experienced professionals, not agents) do the majority of the winning, particularly on the circuits and the clusters, is because their dogs are usually rested, in good weight, and feeling good physically and mentally. They are eating, drinking, and eliminating as they should; and they are not stressed from the heat. Owner-handlers' dogs are typically none of the above. This has nothing to do with politics; it has to do with the fact that most top handlers know how to take proper care of dogs and most owners do not. So let's look at what handlers do and why.

Conditioning

This is one area in which a professional handler has a real edge, since part of the handler's reputation is based on the condition of the dogs in his or her care. Most owner-handlers are unaware of everything that goes into "prime" conditioning.

❖ **If you are a breeder or involved in the world of show dogs, the first step in conditioning is to select a good veterinarian.** This is quite a trick, because really good vets for dog-show people are few and far between.

One problem with vets is us. We expect our vets to be dog people, but they are medical professionals, educated to treat diseases. For example, there is almost no mention in any veterinary class that I know of about whelping puppies. If your vet is not a dog breeder, he or she may never have seen a litter of puppies born. Most students of veterinary medicine are given almost no education on nutrition. Many vets only know what salesmen have told them about dog food and nutrition.

There are no classes in most veterinary schools on structure. There are anatomy classes, which include horses and cows, chickens and pigs, dogs and cats, reptiles, and birds—inside and out. However, anatomy and structure can be two very different things. Most veterinary schools provide no classes on movement. Remember, the title is "School of Veterinary Medicine." Vets are medical professionals, not dog professionals, and there are major empirical distinctions between a "veterinarian" and a "dog person." And both are required for the well-being of show dogs.

What veterinarians are not taught, however, is not the problem. The problem is getting a veterinarian to admit that his or her knowledge of dogs may be limited to pathology, diagnosis, and treatment. The challenge is to find a veterinarian who is open to your knowledge and concerns as a dog person. If you find such a vet, you have found a valuable partner. Take good care of this partner. Pay your bills on time. Remember your vet during the holiday season. A good vet is a real find.

❖ **Every week, each of your dogs should be put on a grooming table.** You have no way of knowing what kind of condition your dogs are in if you don't have your hands on them. You need to check their coats, their weight, their skin, their mouths, their ears, their feet, etc, on a regular basis if you want to keep them in show condition.

Once a problem gets out of hand, the dog looses its show condition. In order to keep dogs in show condition, preventive care is imperative. The key is to stop a problem before it impairs the dog's show career.

❖ **Be cautious about the "virtues" of road work.** My husband and I are opposed to road work as a normal routine for show dogs. Road work is forced exercise with a vehicle at a set speed for a set distance. For most dogs, road work does little or nothing to improve movement.

Road work develops the muscles needed to protect the dog's structure at a certain speed and gait. In short, road work can create generic movement in a show dog. Since different breeds and types of dogs are meant to move in different ways, however, why would we want to train them all to move the same, as if we were striving for "cookie cutter" show dogs? A Bulldog should move like a Bulldog, not like a Clumber Spaniel. A Bearded

Collie should move differently from a German Shepherd. And a Miniature Pinscher would not be a "Min Pin" if it were to lose its unique motion in order to move like a Fox Terrier.

Road work can be good for building stamina and enhancing a dog's attitude. Unfortunately, most people use road work for the purpose of creating better movement in the dog, which seldom works.

❖ **The best way to keep your dogs in condition is to teach them to be loose.** Dogs that run, play, jump, twist, turn, and use all speeds are going to condition their whole bodies so that they can compensate for whatever weakness or structural faults they may have. It's the same principle as athletes cross-training; you never see athletes using just one form of exercise routine.

Just muscling the running gear doesn't compensate for anything. Playing ball and interacting with your dogs are good ways to condition them, because you can watch what they're doing and how.

If you have acreage, offer your dogs free range only at designated times. If they have access to it all the time, their enjoyment of the space will diminish (and dogs can be as lazy as we can be). However, if they live a routine life with only limited times to run loose, they will learn to run their legs off because they will come to know running free as a treat.

Medium-sized and large dogs are usually incapable of moving properly and to their full potential if they spend their lives exercising only in small backyards or paddocks. Dogs need to develop and condition the muscles that move them in straight lines. Running six or ten steps then having to turn a corner won't do it. This also applies to small dogs kept in more confined areas. People tend to scale down available space to fit the size of the dog, so small breeds sometimes end up in the same condition as large dogs exercising in backyards.

So if your dogs spend most of their time in a yard, it is important to take them out for long walks or jogs; find an open space where they can run long, straight distances.

Watering and Elimination

Two of the most important points in maintaining a dog's general health while traveling and showing is to ensure the dog is drinking enough

Chapter 5 / TRICKS OF THE TRADE

water and eliminating regularly.

First, a little lemon juice in the dogs' water is an easy-to-use diuretic. Then, provide the dog ample opportunities to relieve itself.

Learn to use ex-pens for the right reasons. The most common causes of sick dogs at dog shows are that they do not drink enough water and they do not urinate enough. When you put a dog in an ex-pen, give it the opportunity to relieve itself numerous times and to take a drink a dozen times, if it wants.

Dogs at shows should be given a minimum of an hour twice a day in ex-pens. Walks are for relieving boredom and for exercising, but a dog has access to drinking water only before or after a walk. Ex-pens are for drinking, eliminating, and stretching legs–maybe even changing the scenery–but drinking and eliminating are the necessities to meet.

When you're on the road, stick to bottled water if the tap water has an odor. Use it both in watering the dogs and in preparing their food.

If you live in or are traveling to a region inclined toward freezing weather in the winter and you have any outside water buckets, coat the inside of each bucket with margarine or Pam. This will keep the ice from sticking to the bucket, which makes it easier to remove the surface slab of ice each morning. Providing water is useless if the dog is unable to drink it.

In order to help a dog eliminate solid waste regularly when on a show circuit, try "matching" the dog. This involves wetting the sulfur heads of two or three paper matches, then inserting the matches (sulfur end first) into the anus. This is usually just enough of an irritant to where the dog will eliminate in order to expel the matches. The sulfur is nontoxic and almost always works. If matching fails, however, the next thing to try is suppositories for infants. Dogs must eliminate regularly in order to stay in good shape, and it's our responsibility to see that they do.

Back to matching for a moment. Matching is the easiest way to teach dogs to use exercise pens. When ex-pen training, remember that you want to make the dog enjoy show experiences. We dog people sometimes go about teaching in a backwards manner, and ex-pen training is a good example. Typically, we put dogs in an ex-pen, and we wait and wait and wait. Once the dogs eliminate, we reward them by sticking them back in crates. This approach gives dogs little or no reason to eliminate quickly.

In ex-pen training, "match" the dog before putting him or her in the pen; the dog eliminates quickly, you give lots of praise, then the dog gets to stay in the pen as a reward for using it properly.

The same approach should apply for walks. Match the dogs before the walk, praise them for eliminating, then take them for a good long walk as a reward. Eventually, your dogs will eliminate as soon as possible so they can go for a walk.

We have also matched dogs before air travel, which eliminated almost all accidents en route.

Hot-Weather Protection

Many breeds have a difficult time with hot weather. One of the worst things is to keep such a dog in an air-conditioned vehicle at a show, then take it out to perform in an outdoor ring in excessive heat. It isn't great for you either, but it's much worse for the dog.

To minimize the problem, use a fiberglass crate with a metal-grate floor specifically made for that crate. Fill the floor of the crate beneath the metal grate with frozen chemical ice packs. Replace the metal grate so the dogs can't get to the ice packs, then put a blanket or a dog rug on top of the metal grate (because the metal can freeze). Then leave the crate outside in the heat.

The temperature inside the crate can be maintained as much as 20 degrees cooler than the outside temperature; however, the dogs are breathing the air in which they will be running and performing. This helps them avoid the shock of extreme temperature changes before they show. The majority of the dogs who die at shows die because of the heat, and we believe there is absolutely no excuse for it.

One of the most useful inventions I have seen in recent years to combat the effects of hot weather is the battery-powered crate fan. I would use crate fans to protect any heat-sensitive dog in high-temperature situations.

During summer show season, it is helpful to keep an electrolyte supplement on hand. Adding a little in their food will help keep their electrolytes in balance, which will help them handle the stress of hot show trips. The least expensive way to go is to buy the electrolyte solution for poultry—it is sold in most feed stores. For a 50-pound dog, a quarter to a half of a teaspoon in each meal (we feed our dogs twice a day) is sufficient.

You can use Pediolyte (available at any grocery or drug store), but it's much more expensive. Pediolyte is best used when a dog has diarrhea, runs a fever, or is on antibiotics. Add it to their water—a half-and-half mixture—or use it straight. Dogs will be more likely to drink the mixture if you get the unflavored Pediolyte. It works to rebalance their electrolytes, getting their systems back to normal much quicker.

Crates and Air Travel

Our favorite crates for home are furniture crates. Any cabinetmaker can build them to match the rest of your furniture, and they can be used as end tables. The insides are varathaned or finished with Formica for easy cleaning and to resist odor absorbency.

Situate the crates, then have a party at your house and see if anyone notices you have dogs in all of your tables (as long as the dogs are quiet). Also, should you be the only dog person in your home, furniture crates can keep peace with the rest of the family, since they disguise the fact that you have dog crates all over the house. (One crate maker told us his best selling items were crates that doubled as nightstands in bedrooms. Most of us have little space in our bedrooms to add crates, so just make the furniture multi-purpose.)

When you're on the road, the best crates we have found to use are the airline-approved fiberglass crates. It can be scary to take a road trip with dogs in wire crates, due to the fact that the impact of a car accident can break the wires at the welds. At worst, broken wires can impale the dog if they bend inward. At best, the damaged crate can make removing the dog safely very problematic. If you wish to use wire crates for road travel, the safest are crates designed with the smallest space between wires, such as Kennel Aire. These types of wire crates have the least potential for disaster.

When traveling by air, especially during the summer months, avoid transporting dogs in aluminum crates. Heat is the dangerous element here. If you can't touch the outside of a crate on the tarmac of an airport, imagine what the heat buildup is like inside the crate. (This is the only type of crate we have ever seen a seasoned show dog panic in, so our assumption was an intolerable buildup of heat.)

As I mentioned earlier, one of the most exciting products to come on the market in recent years is the battery-operated crate fan. It is capable of moving an enormous amount of air and attaches securely to the outside of the crate door. Personally, I would never fly another dog without one of these fans on the crate. (It's also invaluable for road trips, as you can purchase an adapter that plugs into the cigarette lighter, so it can provide airflow throughout long days on the road and still be operational for any emergency.)

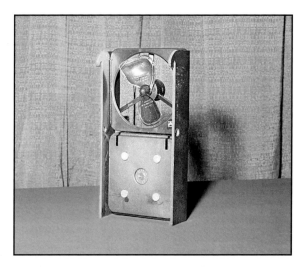

Figure 5-07: Crate fan

The average exhibitor is destined to fly with dogs to at least two shows—Westminister and the National Specialty (and it is wise for all exhibitors to make these shows as often as possible). For airline travel, the only thing you need to put in the dog's crate before a flight is paper towels. It takes three rolls to fill a 400-size crate.

This is a good job for your kids or your neighbor's kids, because each sheet needs to be torn off the roll and thrown in the crate one at a time. Just toss the sheets in and let them fall as they may. The trick then is convincing the dogs to go in the crates, because they won't think there's any room left for them.

As soon as they go in, nose around, and circle a couple of times, they find it quite comfortable. Paper towels are excellent insulation against both heat and cold. Moreover, when you fly a dog, there is always the chance that the dog may have an accident. A normal, clean-living house dog who has an accident in its crate will usually spend the rest of the trip trying to bury it. They can bury their "accidents" in paper towels without any damage to the leather on their noses or to any other part of their bodies. Also, they rarely get any of the "accident" on themselves, due to the absorbency of the paper towels. (This is also a great approach when transporting puppies by air.)

In your carry-on baggage, pack a plastic garbage bag. When you land, if the dog has made a mess, put the paper towels in the garbage bag, which you deposit in the nearest trash receptacle at the airport. Carry the dog's regular blanket in your luggage and use it in the crate after arrival and for the trip home. It is of no competitive concern if the dog skins its nose or makes a mess once you're homeward bound.

Before you fly with your dog, contact the American Dog Owners Association (ADOA) for the most current information about travel crates (see Resources section of this book). Priscilla Benkin does an enormous amount of research to help keep our dogs safe in air travel, and the ADOA publishes her reports.

Be aware that the airlines are tightening their cargo regulations. To find out what the most current regulations are, you can call (301) 734-7833. They will send you a copy of the current rules. Air travel is becoming more problematic because of the inconsistencies in how regulations are interpreted. One woman flying to the Doberman National was prohibited from flying her dog in even a 700-size crate because the airline personnel would not allow the dog to fly in a crate in which even the dog's ears touched the crate ceiling.

The most current air travel regulations state that a dog must be able to stand up and turn around comfortably in its crate. What the airlines seem to be unaware of is the risk posed by a spacious crate when a dog is flying. Too much space means the dogs may fall during take-offs or landings and injure themselves.

We want our dogs to be most comfortable laying down—the safest position they can be in during a flight. Be that as it may, the main point is to be prepared for different interpretations when you enter the airport. Flexibility and adaptability will keep your blood pressure down and keep the airlines amiable toward all of us who fly with our dogs.

Collars and Leads

There is a sound reason for everything that a good handler does. Take the issue of leads and collars.

It doesn't matter what you show dogs on after they understand what you ask and expect of them. However, the easiest way to teach show dogs what you want and expect, without being set up to make mistakes, is to teach them on a choke chain.

All collars cause coat damage, but the collar that causes the most damage is the obedience-type choke chain with rings linked together. Everytime you pull on this kind of choke, any hair that gets caught between the rings will break or be cut. Choke chains known as snake, jeweled, hexagon, etc, will do the least amount of coat damage.

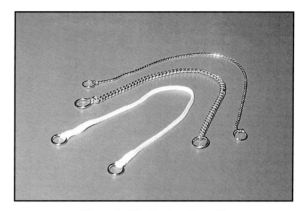

Figure 5-08: Chokes (L to R): nylon, obedience, snake

Teach with a choke chain (preferably nylon), but be sure you know how to position and use it correctly.

1. Put the collar on as an obedience collar. That means the ring attached to the lead is over the back of the neck, with the lead on the righthand side of the dog.

2. With the collar rings and lead held in your left hand between the dog's ears, use the index finger of your right hand to pull the collar forward under the chin as far as it will go. While you are still holding on lightly under the chin, pull the collar up and back with your left hand. This will position the collar around the

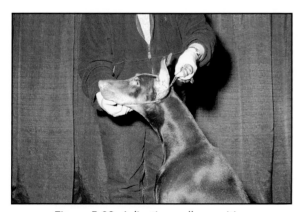

Figure 5-09: Adjusting collar position

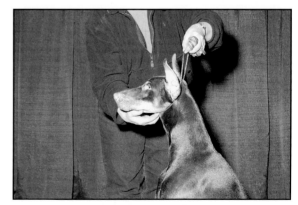

Figure 5-10: Setting collar position

bone structure of the head almost in the same fashion as you would pick up a puppy in a suspended position (see Chapter 2: Puppy Evaluations).

3. Once you have the collar correctly positioned, the dog will accept your control and understand you are the boss. From this point on, just repositioning the collar will remind the dog that you are in charge. While you are teaching the dog this concept, reward immediately when the dog responds the way you want.

Although a nylon choke chain is more damaging to the dog's coat (nylon causes static and static breaks hair), it is still my choice for teaching, because it is much easier to keep in position. Once the lesson is over, however, remove the nylon choke. It is advisable to avoid using any kind of nylon collar as a show dog's daily collar, since it will do enormous damage to the coat. If you are going to leave a collar on the dog, a rolled-leather collar does the least amount of damage.

When you are teaching, we recommend using only leather leads. Any other kind of lead can burn or cut your hand if it scrapes across your skin, and you're more likely to let go of the lead should that happen. Leather is the safest, most reliable lead to use for teaching purposes.

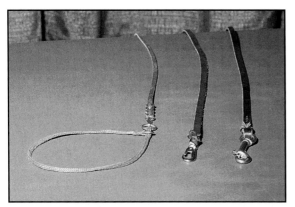

Figure 5-11: Show lead, blade snap, and bolt snap

If you're going to use a leather lead with a snap on it, use a lead with a blade snap to ensure you're not going to lose your dog in the process of its education. A bolt-type snap can and does open accidentally.

Our favorite show leads have no snaps on them. They are permanently attached to the collar and they have a swivel, so the lead remains untangled without any work on your part.

Bait

If you are going to bait a dog, the bait to use is liver (or another type of organ meat). Buy frozen-sliced liver (found in the grocer's freezer section), so each piece is the same thickness all the way through.

1. Put the liver—either frozen or thawed—in a pan of water heavily salted with garlic salt. Boil the liver on the stove while you preheat your oven to 350 degrees.

2. Once you've cooked it for awhile (long enough to let the garlic salt penetrate), take it off the stove and rinse the liver in cold-running water, thoroughly cleaning it to eliminate any residue from the boiling. Set three or four layers of paper towels on a cookie sheet, and put the liver on the paper towels.

3. Turn your preheated oven to "Off," then put the cookie sheet in the oven so the liver can dry. It takes the same amount of time to dry the outside of the liver (while keeping the inside moist and flavorful) as it does to cool your oven. The garlic salt helps to preserve the liver, thus preventing sliminess and stomach upsets. Warning: Never put paper in a stove that is "On."

If you're going someplace where you may not have access to refrigeration or a cooler, freeze the cooked liver in baggies (a couple of slices per bag) while it is still warm. Before you start out on your trip, take the baggie containing the frozen liver out of the freezer and fill it with rock salt. As the liver thaws, it will absorb the salt, which in turn helps to preserve it. This will keep the liver good for about one week. Before you use the liver, however, remember to wash it thoroughly, as it would be extremely salty otherwise.

The reasons to use liver are:

- ❖ Almost all dogs like it.
- ❖ It is one of the least messy baits to use.
- ❖ The garlic salt encourages dogs to drink more water, which makes them urinate more, which keeps them healthier on the road.
- ❖ Liver is one of the highest sources of energy.

When we have correctly used liver bait, every dog we have handled or worked with has been enthusiastic about it and has done well on it. Of course, there are always exceptions to every rule, but the odds are good that liver bait will succeed for you. However, learn to distinguish between bait and food or treats.

Avoid carrying bait in your hand while moving the dog around the ring. Bait in hand may wrongly encourage your dog to sidewind. At the same time, never tease your dog with an empty hand. Your dog must always be able to trust you and believe in you.

Bait is given only when dogs do something for it, and bait is only given in very small portions. It is used to reinforce a dog's behavior when it meets the expectations of the exhibitor.

Honing the Show Attitude

The next concept is difficult to grasp and even more difficult to practice, but it can pay off. It is one of the major advantages that professional handlers have over owner-handlers. No matter how spoiled your dogs are at home (and I am a firm believer that dogs should be spoiled), when you get in your vehicle to go to a show, learn to ignore your dogs. What you want to teach them is that they will get your undivided attention only in the ring.

If you take your dogs to the park, and they go to McDonald's for lunch, and they sleep on the bed, why in Heaven's name would they want to go to a dog show? But if they're sleeping in crates and being properly taken care of but not pampered or catered to until show time, then the dogs will usually be willing to give you 110 percent, because they learn to look forward to all of the attention that you are going to give them at that time. (A dog should spend only as much time in a crate as it normally spends sleeping. Other hours should be spent exercising, feeding, and working with the dog.)

You will be astonished what a difference this kind of approach can make in the show attitude of a dog. And dogs adapt very quickly. When dogs of one breed are travelling with a handler, they even learn which dogs they follow as each is taken out for showing. You can see their excitement: "Oh boy, I'm next!" It is one of the reasons dogs with professional handlers usually show better than dogs with their owner-handlers.

MISCELLANEOUS TIPS

The following are random morsels of wisdom we have gathered along our way. I offer them here as food for thought:

❖ **If you're a breeder and you always name litters with easily recognizable theme names, it gains you years of peer recognition.** When people put puppies together with your kennel name, all of a sudden they know who you are and what you breed. This is a great help to breeders, especially those just starting.

❖ **When you have a bitch that is due to whelp, add a little bit of baking soda to all water she has access to a day or so before whelping.** It helps to neutralize acid milk, so a little baking soda can really help reduce the chance of colicky puppies.

❖ **If you use exercise pens, get the cheapest ones you can find.** The more expensive pens are made of heavier-guage wire; every time you set them up and take them down, the welding is compromised. We have found that the cheapest ones are more lightweight, more flexible, and more durable.

The best snaps to use to connect ex-pens are the brass snaps. They will not corrode in weather; other metals used for snaps can corrode eventually to where they will not close properly, and accidents happen.

❖ **If you use water buckets, make sure you put the bucket on a line instead of snapping it to something solid.** If the bucket is hooked to something solid and the dog gets caught, it can drown. If the bucket is hooked to a line and the dog gets caught, all it has to do is move and water will come out of the bucket.

❖ **If you are going to use ex-pens, invest in a sunscreen.** If you put a plastic tarp over an ex-pen, it can increase the heat in the pen. A sunscreen allows for airflow underneath it while reducing the direct sun.

❖ **When it comes to pooper scoopers, buy the cheapest you can buy.** The cheaper they are, the more flexible they are, the longer they last.

Chapter 5 / TRICKS OF THE TRADE

❖ **You have perhaps heard the expression that a dog can feel your tension going down the lead.** There may be some truth to that, but it is true that a dog can smell adrenalin. When you are nervous, your dog can sniff it on you. One way to help counteract this is to carry breath mints with you when you're showing, and pop a breath mint every time you walk in the ring. This is also a good idea for judges, since judges can be nervous in that ring, too, and the dogs will know it. If they sense anxiety, it can make them anxious.

❖ **When traveling in an RV, it is infinitely safer for your dogs as well as for the environment to use a capful of fabric softener in the toilet instead of toilet chemicals.** Toilet chemicals can be toxic. Also, RV toilet paper is single ply, has no perfume, and is undyed. Perfumes are what make toilet paper hard to break down, so if you buy regular single-ply toilet paper without dyes or perfumes, you are getting the same quality of biodegradable paper as you would be getting with RV toilet paper but for less money.

One brief aside: When your RV is plugged in at home, regularly check the water level of the battery. A battery can use up to 50 percent more water when it is plugged in than when it's running.

❖ **The best choice in food and water dishes for your dogs is stainless steel, glass, or crockery.** Chemicals used in processing plastics can break down with age and leak into the water, which can cause the pigment on a dog's nose to fade. This effect seems to be reversible only about half the time.

❖ **Anyone with dogs also has flies.** If you plant marigolds underneath all of your windows, around your kennel and all of your doors, flies will not come in. Flies will not fly over or around the scent of marigolds.

❖ **For outdoor dog beds, make your own.** Start with No. 9 or No. 10 white-duck canvas (remnants are the cheapest way to go) and four 2x4's, 2x6's, or 2x8's (height is dependent on the weight of your dogs). Make a frame that fits whatever size piece of canvas you bought.

Nail the canvas (use only roofing nails) on the top edge of the frame. If you nail the canvas over onto the side of the frame, it will come loose the first time a dog chews on a corner of the frame.

This kind of bed does not damage coat or hold fleas. If the canvas is not heavy duty, however, dogs will quickly find themselves unsure of their footing, so they will be less likely to use the bed. The cotton canvas will reshrink every time you hose off the bed, thus keeping it tight, like a trampoline.

Figure 5-12: Homemade dog bed

The cost for a size that can accommodate an adult Doberman is approximately $10 to $20, and the bed will last for years. We have some that have lasted over 15 years. These are great beds to use in doghouses, because it will keep the dog off the ground.

❖ **Cedar chips or shavings are unadvisable in some circumstances.** Cedar stains when it gets wet, which can spell disaster for white dogs. Also, puppies can get quite ill if they eat cedar. So for white dogs or puppies, choose another type of bedding material.

❖ **Skunk odors are most easily dealt with by washing the dog down with liquid fabric softener.** Tomato juice works, but oh, the mess! Have you ever poured tomato juice on a dog whose first inclination is to shake when dowsed with any kind of liquid? Suddenly, you have an art deco washroom. And vinegar works well, but oh, the smell–for days.

The least disruptive option we have found is to kill the odor with straight fabric softener, give the dog a regular bath, then spray it down with diluted fabric softener.

Another option, if you happen to have the supplies, is to bathe the dog with a solution made up of 1 quart of hydrogen peroxide (3 percent) mixed together with 1/4 cup of baking soda and 1 teaspoon of liquid dish soap. Mix in a bucket, then saturate the dog's coat with the solution, using a sponge. Once saturated, bathe the dog.

❖ **It can be risky to use any pine products in your housecleaning, if you have dogs.** Most pine products are made with concentrated pine oil, which can be toxic to a dog's liver. Even scrubbing the kitchen floor with a pine product can be dangerous; the dog walks across the floor, and later licks its feet.

This routine can cause a buildup of the pine oil, and you run the risk of the dog developing liver problems later in life. You needn't worry about pine cones, pine shavings, or pine boughs, since they do not contain concentrated oils.

❖ **Carpet fresheners have been known to cause a toxic reaction in dogs, so avoid using them if you have carpeting in your house.**

❖ **If you are staying in hotels or motels, first thing to do is to close the toilet lid.** Public accommodations may use chemicals in the toilet that can kill dogs.

❖ **One of the easiest ways to improve coat condition is to use a humidifier in whatever room your dogs spend the most time, be it a bedroom, the kitchen, or a kennel.** Even in humid areas, most homes and kennels are heated and air-conditioned, which generally removes the greater measure of humidity in the air.

❖ **If you have show dogs, it's a good idea to also have an aloe vera plant in your house.** The natural enzymes of the slimy insides works incredibly well to heal cut pads. Even a pad that is cut severely enough to where your vet recommends wrapping it and keeping the dog off of the foot can be healed in a matter of a few days if you use aloe vera. But it must be directly from the plant.

There are many aloe vera products on the market, most of which are totally ineffectual, because processing destroys the enzymes that speed healing. In our experience, aloe vera is only miraculous in healing cut pads, although it can be helpful in other situations.

❖ **Aspirin, applied to the skin, can work wonders on lick sores.** For lick sores, or lick granulomas, apply a greasy substance, such as Vaseline or Neosporin ointment. Crush an aspirin and sprinkle the power on the greased surface. Then wrap the area with VetWrap, and leave it for three days. The wound will fill in, and the dog will leave it alone.

❖ **If you have a bitch that's due to come in season, you can save yourself a lot of hassle with males by giving the bitch chlorophyll tablets just before and during her heat.** (Human brands are usually much less expensive than brands for dogs.) A 50-pound dog would get two pills twice a day. The chlorophyll prevents the odor from permeating the air. A male allowed to smell her or her urine will know, but you won't have males coming from miles around to park themselves on your doorstep for three weeks.

If you're going to breed her, take her off of the pills a couple of days before the breeding. After all, you wouldn't want to teach a stud dog to associate the smell of chlorophyll with a bitch in season.

❖ **If you have a male who is ultrasensitive to bitches in season, or has an excessive interest in sniffing the ground, randomly put vanilla extract on his nose and whiskers (if he has whiskers).** A dog usually cannot smell through the odor of vanilla. It has to be done randomly at home, so he just thinks you're nuts and this is just one of the things you do to him.

Keep the vanilla in your tack box so that every time you go to a dog show, vanilla on the nose is simply part of the normal grooming procedure you go through for a show; that way, the dog's concentration will be undisturbed by any bitches in season at the show. Vanilla is long lasting and non-irritating. Other products, such as menthol or Vicks, can irritate them and are short lived.

Common sense is the key to all you do. If you are doing advanced obedience with your dog, common sense tells us the dog is going to need his olfactory prowess for such an activity. Therefore, the use of vanilla is ridiculous in this case.

❖ **Many dogs, particularly males, develop a urine odor that seems to hang around the dog whether it's urinating or not.** First, check to make

Chapter 5 / TRICKS OF THE TRADE

sure there is no medical reason for this. If the dog is healthy, the acid content in their system may be a possible cause. Altering the acid content of their system—higher or lower—will, in most cases, eliminate the odor. The easiest thing to try is Vitamin C; you can try vinegar, but Vitamin C is easier. An antacid works well on toy dogs, but large breeds would require incredibly large doses.

❖ **Charcoal tablets for people (available in most drug stores) are very useful for dogs with gas.** The only drawback is that charcoal absorbs not only gas but any oral medications the dog might be on. So avoid using charcoal if your dogs are on oral medication.

❖ **If your dogs enjoy chewing on wood, an easy thing to try is to spread a paste of water and alum (used to put the pucker in pickles) on any wood the dogs gnaw on outside.** The paste is messy, so it's best to use it only outside. Once the dog tastes the alum, he or she will generally stop chewing wood altogether.

It is imperative that you do everything you can to prevent your dogs from chewing on pressure-treated wood (used for fencing and decking). Most such wood is treated with arsenic, which can have a horrible effect on dogs.

❖ **If you have dog houses or dog beds in your kennel runs, make sure the houses or beds are situated near the gate.** Dogs have a tendency to eliminate as far away from where they sleep as possible. With the house or bed near the gate, eliminations will be at the other end of the run.

This idea comes under the heading of making your work as easy as possible. Who needs feces right in front of the run entrance to be spread around by opening the gate and having the dogs run through it to jump on you in a glorious, albeit odoriferous and messy, greeting?

❖ **About stacking and showing:** Most people have difficulty stacking the front legs far enough under the dog; all of us have a tendency to stack the front legs too far forward (and many show photographers encourage it). There is a simple solution. Hold the lead in your right hand, cup your left hand against the dog's left upper arm (the edge of your hand should be at the dog's leg joint), bend the upper arm, and let the leg fall gently in a normal fashion. The leg will set down where it should be. Then simply fix the dog's right leg in alignment with the left. This sets an appropriate stacking pattern for the dog.

One note about dogs that are stacked on tables. Please, avoid picking your dog up by its tail. The tail is part of the spine. Pulling a terrier out of a hole by its tail is pulling in the natural direction of the spine; thus, it poses no risk of harm. Lifting a terrier, or other breed, onto a table by its tail is pulling the tail perpendicular to the natural direction of the spine. Why take an unnecessary risk?

Never back a dog up in the show ring. Dogs always move cow-hocked when they are backed up, so it will only succeed in showing the judge a fault the dog may not actually possess.

Also, keep the dog's head straight forward while a judge is examining it. When a dog's head is turned, its shoulders feel worse to the judge's hand than they actually are when the head is straight forward.

When you are in the ring, keep in mind that if your dogs look like it is their idea to be there, they will give a greater show appearance than if they look like you are making them be there.

TIPS FOR THE DOG-SHOW NOVICE

Remember, all of us have been where you are now—beginners or novices trying to find our way in the show world, while simultaneously trying to look like we fit in and know what we're doing. Be assured that the majority of experienced dog-show people are willing to be helpful and supportive, in return for those who were there for them when they were new to the sport. You enter the Fancy with one common bond to all others—a love of dogs.

❖ **If you are just beginning as an owner-handler, the first thing you need to know is this: The left side of the dog is always the show side.** This is the side the judge will always see in the ring.

❖ **Any owner-handler should be showing at Canadian Kennel Club (CKC), United Kennel Club (UKC), States Kennel Club (SKC), or

Chapter 5 / TRICKS OF THE TRADE

International shows, or whatever else might be available to you in your area. You only gain confidence by winning. All of these shows are more informal, more relaxed, and slower-paced than AKC shows. Also, professional handlers are less likely to be in force at these events, so your chances of winning more frequently are better. If you can go to these shows, you'll have a more comfortable environment in which to learn not only how to show your dog but also how to win, and that will increase your chances of winning when you come back to the AKC shows.

❖ **Read all you can—learn all you can.** The more information you have, the more you will use your own discrimination about how best to care for your dogs, how best to go about planning your breeding program. The more your read, study, and learn, the more variety of opinions and information you will take in. And just like your dog can be taught to learn, we can learn to think. There is an annotated bibliography at the end of this book to get you started.

❖ **Become so familiar with your show lead that you no longer think about it.** Pick a place in your house where you frequently sit, be it your favorite television chair or telephone chair. Fasten the show lead to the left front leg of that chair. Then, everytime you sit there, pick up the lead and practice folding it in and out of your hand, until you stop thinking about how to do it.

Next, fasten some keys to your show lead, and practice running with the lead, reeling it in and out, until you do it without rattling the keys. This exercise will teach you balance and smoothness of motion.

❖ **Do not enter in the Novice Class.** When you're a novice, you need to be in one of the larger classes. This allows you more time to watch experienced exhibitors and learn. The Novice Class is usually small and offers little in the way of experience to study.

❖ **One of the fastest ways to increase your knowledge about movement is to go to the Doberman ring and watch.** Almost always the breed has a decent entry; the dogs are tall enough to where you can really watch the legs; there is no hair or color or patterns to cause optical illusions when they move; it is a breed shown, for the most part, hands off; and the quality of Dobermans is generally very high. For these reasons, you generally can learn a lot by watching Dobermans move in the ring.

❖ **In order to spend money wisely when showing dogs, it's important to learn how to group your shows.** Sit down and figure out how many shows you can afford to enter in a year. If you can afford to go to 12 shows a year, and you go to one per month, you may never finish your dog, because every time you walk into the show ring, it's a new experience for you and for the dog, and you're both nervous and don't quite know what's going on.

If you can go to 12 show per year and decide to do a three-day weekend four times a year, it can make a major difference in your ability to win. The first day, you get the nervousness out of the way; the second day, you're getting it together; by the third day, the odds are in your favor. By grouping your shows, then, you increase your chances of winning.

❖ **If you are willing do the kind of work that a professional handler does to prepare for a show, you as an owner-handler have the edge over professional handlers the majority of the time.** Good judges are always on the lookout for new dogs. And when you only have one dog, while a handler may have 10 to 20 dogs to keep track of, you have a significant advantage—time and focus. Make the most of this advantage in your grooming, choice of clothing, support, etc.

❖ **I am a firm believer in stewarding at shows.** Being a ring steward, you can learn that much more about the workings of the show ring; it gives you an opportunity to pay back a bit of what shows have given you; and if there are two dogs in the ring of equal quality, the judge just might point to the dog handled by someone familiar. That's not politics; that's human nature. Stewarding is also a great way to network.

Chapter 5 / TRICKS OF THE TRADE

One last thought along the lines of dog wherewithal: We are firm in our belief that dogs should be allowed to be dogs. We have dogs because we love dogs. An artificial or sterile life is not much of a life—not for a person or a dog. Let them be what they were born to be.

*Be prepared: You never get a second chance
to make a first impression.*

grooming for show and health

The more a dog has the look of a show dog, the greater its chances of winning. Moreover, since grooming is an integral part of maintaining a dog's health, it may help to prevent or at least minimize unnecessary problems. For these reasons, grooming is an essential element not only in the sport of purebred dogs but also in the ownership of any dog.

Anyone who is a judge or anyone who wants to be a judge needs to know what can be accomplished with great grooming. It is my belief that grooming should be part of a judge's education—that a Poodle judge should at least know the names of the various coat patterns and a Terrier judge should be familiar with the process of coat stripping and what is involved in maintaining a hard-coated Terrier.

I also believe that the best-groomed dogs at a dog show should be the obedience and agility dogs. The obedience and agility dogs are, after all, the ones the public watches. When the public approaches those rings, what do they see? Oftentimes, they see dogs so lacking in presentation as to do a disservice to the breeds those dogs represent.

Breeders can do so much to help and teach obedience and agility exhibitors how to properly groom the dogs they are going to show. When these exhibitors invest more in the presentation of their dogs, they invest more in the presentation of themselves in the ring, which raises their status in the show world.

Chapter 6 / TRICKS OF THE TRADE

ATTENTION TO THE BASICS

For shows, you and the dog need to look the part, be it in conformation, obedience, or agility. We are the custodians of our sport, and the public should be able to look to us for guidance by example. We are the ones who can educate, inform, and enlighten the public, and the impression we make at shows and exhibitions can work for or against the dog world as a whole.

Nail Care

One of the worst things we can do is neglect our dogs' nails. If you want to know what long nails on a dog's feet feel like, let your nails grow past your fingertips, then go pull weeds by hand for a few hours. Or let your toenails grow to where they press against the inside of your shoes. As a dog's nails begin to bear down on the ground, the dog's foot will stretch, spread, or turn to avoid the discomfort. Prolonged neglect may result in the tendons of the feet stretching to such an extent that the foot flattens. The damage is irreparable. No dog should have to endure this avoidable structural harm.

Very few dogs resent having their nails done. What they resent is the fight over nail care. So, don't fight them. Put them on a grooming table, with a noose securely around the base of their head, and stack them comfortably. Then, do the nails. If the dogs fight, don't fight back. Stop and reposition them, then start again. When they realize you aren't going to fight with them, they will usually settle down. (A severe structural weakness or injury are the most common exceptions to this rule.)

I am a firm believer in grinding nails, as opposed to cutting nails. When grinding, it is better to use the sandpaper cylinders rather than a stone. Stones can get very hot and subsequently cause discomfort. Using the finest grit of sanding bands will eliminate bouncing and reduce vibration against the dog's foot. If done correctly, grinding can actually help train a nail shorter, so each time you grind the nails, you can grind them back a little farther. Cutting the nails way back, on the other hand, can risk an infection in the toe bone.

The bottom of a dog's nail looks like the bottom of a horse hoof. It has a fleshy center (the sole); it has a protective ridge all the way around it (the wall); somewhere in or near the center of the sole is the quick.

The only way to encourage the dog's nails to recede is to use a grinder to take back the protective wall of the nail from underneath, until the bottom of the nail is smooth as glass. Doing this nearly exposes the sole (but not to the point of hurting the dog), which then will recede every time something (eg, grass, concrete, gravel) touches it . Each time you grind the nails after that, you will generally be able to take more of the wall back.

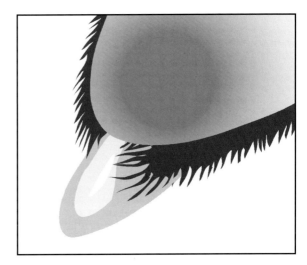

Figure 6-01: Dog nail from underside

In order to train nails back, all of the nails need to be done from the rear of the leg. When working on the dog's hind foot, hold the leg straight back. Holding the leg out sideways can cause discomfort, and the dog will resist. Grind down the underside of each nail until it is smooth. Then, grind the length of it in a straight line to the edge of the sole, rounding it if you prefer.

Avoid struggling. Remember, manhandling will make matters worse by encouraging the dog to resort to panic. A helping hand can be useful to support the dog or to help limit resistance, but forcibly holding the dog in place will prolong the struggle.

A colleague who presents an excellent handling seminar around the country believes clipping the nails is preferable to grinding. What fascinates me about this is that his reason is exactly the same as my reason for using a grinder—a prime example of why people should do what works for them.

The best approach is to start familiarizing the dog with nail care when it is very young, while you still have the advantage.

If your dogs resist nail care, remember sometimes things that are good for all of us may feel less than pleasurable. It doesn't mean you shouldn't do them, though. If a child hates getting shots, do we let them go unvaccinated? You owe it to your show dogs to keep them in good condition, right down to their toes.

Bathing

The fundamentals of a great show coat are: (1) genetics, (2) appropriate food, and (3) correct coat work and cleaning. Dirt and build-up can damage a dog's coat, so bathing is a necessary element in the care we give our dogs.

One of the most important elements of bathing show dogs, no matter what the breed, to is wash them with free-flowing water. Water shooting out of any kind of nozzle can twist and damage hair on a coated dog and reduce the natural oils in a smooth-coated dog's skin.

Use only dog shampoo, and be sure to dilute it according to the directions. The pH balance for dogs is different than that of humans, so using a human shampoo can adversely affect the dog's coat and skin.

The way I used to test shampoos when my husband and I were handling was to first wash the motor home with the shampoo. It was the easiest way to find out how well it cut grease and grime, how easy it rinsed, what kind of a film it left, and what kind of damage it did to my hands after being in it for an hour or so. I'm sure the theory still holds true.

Insofar as conditioners are concerned, don't use one unless the dog's coat needs it. There seems to be no one conditioner that is right for all coat types and conditions; the best thing to do is to talk with your peers, particularly those whose dogs have the best coats, to find out what works for them. Be careful not to add too much oil to the coat, as oil attracts dirt, and dirt is one of the most damaging elements to a dog's coat.

When bathing a show dog, it is very important to learn to wash only the hair. Unless the dog has a specific skin disorder, the skin should be left alone in the bathing process. Dogs need their natural oils to maintain good coat condition. Getting down to the skin, like we get down and scrub our scalps, strips the natural oils away.

You can bathe a dog every day of its life without damaging the coat, as long as you bathe the coat and leave the skin alone. Removing a healthy dog's necessary oils on a regular basis will impair the health of the skin (and coat).

Always bathe a show dog with the lay of the hair. Moreover, never pour shampoo along the topline. It may collect in the hair follicles, making it very difficult to rinse out completely. The dog may appear to have dandruff after a day or two, but it is actually the dried shampoo coming loose from the follicles.

For a smooth-coated dog, pour your shampoo onto a dampened net body sponge (the kind used with liquid body soaps for humans) or a regular sponge, then brush the sponge over the coat in the direction the hair lies. For a coated dog, put the shampoo on a dampened net body sponge or pick the hair up in your hand and pour the shampoo onto the hair.

Avoid scouring the hair; use the palm of your hand instead of your fingers. With long hair, knead the shampoo in as if you were washing a fine sweater. Rinse and towel-dry with the lay of the hair, and when you rinse, be sure to rinse out all of the soap. Then, towel-dry with the lay of the hair.

Dryers

When it comes to dryers, you must have a stand dryer if you have coated breeds with a drop coat (eg, Bearded Collies, Afghans, Malteses). Stand dryers are expensive, but with these kinds of breeds, you have no choice if you want specials-quality hair. It takes two hands to properly dry hair that hangs; this doesn't leave a hand free with which to hold a dryer. With other coated breeds (eg, Golden Retrievers, Belgian Sheepdogs, Siberian Huskies, Pomeranians), you can get by with a forced-air or hand-held dryer. However, stand dryers are the best option and worth every penny you pay for them.

COAT CARE

The trick to great grooming (with the possible exception of Poodles and Bichons) is to make it look like God grew it that way. All grooming should be done on a table in front of a mirror, so you have the view of what the judge is going to see.

For proper coat care, it's imperative to use the right tools on the right coats. Tools we will discuss in the following sections are:

- ❖ Pin brush.
- ❖ Slicker.
- ❖ Stainless steel comb.
- ❖ Blade brush.

Chapter 6 / TRICKS OF THE TRADE

Figure 6-02: Rake (above), pin brush, slicker, stainless steel comb, and blade brush.

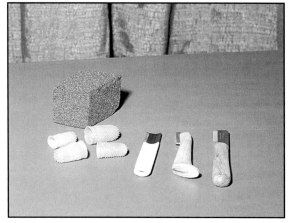

Figure 6-03: Pumice stone, rubber fingers, and assorted stripping knives.

❖ Rake.
❖ Rubber fingers.
❖ Stripping knives.
❖ Pumice stone.

About Dog Hair

Perhaps you have heard a term used by Terrier people: "Rolling the coat." This means to remove a portion of the dog's coat on a regular basis. When rolling a coat, Terrier people pull the longest hairs on a continual basis, so that new coat is always coming in. In this way, Terriers can be kept in show coat all year round. If done regularly, a show Terrier will have many levels of coat at any given time—the longest hair ready to be pulled, the medium length in its prime, and the shortest length or the new coat emerging.

In many respects, this process applies to all breeds. Each hair follicle holds only one guard hair. It may contain up to thousands of undercoat hairs, but only one guard hair. There is nothing you can do, shy of drugs or spaying/neutering, that will prevent a dog from blowing its undercoat (if it has one). However, you can control the blowing of the top coat or guard hairs. If the guard hair is kept thick and healthy, you can keep almost all dogs in show condition, even when the dogs are blowing their undercoat.

Dog hair grows in cycles, while human hair grows continuously. Except for a few hairs that are constantly falling out in our houses, the dead guard hairs stay in their repsective follicles until a new cycle begins. The new growth pushes the old hair out. The natural shedding process will leave a dog out of show condition until the new coat comes in. This is the process you can control.

When hair dies, it loses both its shine and intensity of color. Therefore, if you learn to remove the dead hair regularly, the coat will retain its shine and deeper color—without having to use any cosmetic enhancers. The more things you put on hair, the more hair is damaged and the faster it dies.

Since new hair pushes out the old hair as it surfaces, dead hair stays in place, waiting for the next cycle. However, when you remove dead hair before it is ready to shed naturally, new growth is immediately stimulated. Thus, the more dead hair you remove in regular grooming sessions, the more new growth is constantly in progress and the greater the chances of the dog remaining in show condition.

Each type of coat needs to be "rolled" in a different fashion.

Drop-Coated Breeds

The first required tool for drop-coated breeds is a pin brush. Make sure the pin brush you get has metal pins in a rubber base. Plastic or nylon cause static, and static breaks hair. Use brushes with metal bristles only, and no knobs on the ends of the bristles. The more flexible the side motion of the bristles, the less damage it will cause to the hair.

For breeds requiring brushing, you will also have need of a slicker. The slicker is used on all feet up to the stop pad in front and up to the hock joint in back. Foot hair is a different texture than the rest of the coat and is more effectively separated with a slicker than with a pin brush. I have found that a long-handled, smaller slicker is preferable, because it has better balance so it is more properly used.

Teach the dog to lay down on the table. This means you must lay the dog in the position you want, as opposed to the position the dog might want (for example, the dog may want to lay in such a way as to hide an area it doesn't want you to brush). Stand it on the table, embrace it around the far elbow and knee, draw the dog into your body, then lay it gently on its side, keeping your body on the dog until it relaxes in this position.

Chapter 6 / TRICKS OF THE TRADE

Figure 6-04: Shih Tzu

Figure 6-05: Yorkshire Terrier

Figure 6-06: Afghan Hound

Laying the dog on the table to brush it is the only way you can keep a long-coated dog in good show coat. Every hair needs to be brushed against the lay. This is the only way to remove dead hair before it is ready to fall out, and removing dead hair stimulates new growth. If you brush with the lay of the hair, you will only be removing hair that has already begun shedding. And brushing against the lay is problematic if your dog is standing. You'll find yourself brushing against gravity, which will tire your arm quickly and make for a less than thorough job.

Never brush hair that is dry, since this will cause static and static breaks hair. Also, laying a dog down on a carpeted surface to brush it can pull static from the carpet into the coat. Always mist the hair before brushing it. However, brush wet hair only when using a dryer on it. Wet hair stretches and weakens when brushed, but brushing with a dryer relieves tension on the hair.

Mist over the coat with water or whatever you find works best for your breed, then line-brush the coat (make a line at the skin and brush one line of hair at a time) lightly enough that you do not hear the brush going through the coat. Remember, every hair is brushed against the lay. Keep the motion in the wrist and brush the hair from the skin all the way to the end of the hair.

After you have brushed every hair against the lay, stand the dog up and rebrush the coat in the pattern appropriate for the breed. You may also go through the coat at this stage with a stainless steel comb to ensure all loose hair has been removed.

When using a comb, put it into the coat perpendicular to the body. Putting a comb into the coat at an angle can tear out hair. Use a slicker on its feet and on all short-coated areas (always against the lay first).

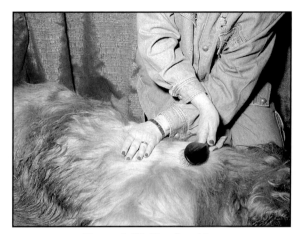

Figure 6-07: Line-brushing

Powder the coat in areas where something is caught in the hair, be it seeds, twigs, or brambles. Baby powder works well. The powder will coat whatever is stuck in the hair, then you can brush through that area without ripping hair out. If there is urine in the coat, the best option is to bathe that area before brushing it, but powdering it does help.

Smooth-Coated Breeds

All it takes to keep a smooth-coated dog's coat in show condition is a chamois and a pumice stone. A pumice stone, used lightly with the lay of the hair, will remove the dead hair in the same fashion that brushing a coated breed against the lay does.

When using a pumice stone, scrape it along a hard surface first to round off the sharp edges. Run it along the coat in a rolling fashion to avoid cutting any of the hair. Make sure the skin is pulled taut over any area where the skin is wrinkled, plump, or loose.

Figure 6-08: Dalmatian

Chapter 6 / TRICKS OF THE TRADE

Figure 6-09: Great Dane

Figure 6-10: Doberman Pinscher

"Stoning" a smooth-coated breed in this fashion once or twice a week keeps the coat lustrous and rich in color, while considerably reducing the amount of shedding the dog does in the house.

After stoning, soak a good-quality chamois in hot water, ring it out well, then wipe down the dog. The chamois removes any residue left from the pumice stone, and the natural oil in the cloth will leave the coat wonderfully shiny, thus eliminating the need for additional products to make the coat look good.

A smooth-coated dog should go into the ring looking smooth; in other words, there should be no hairs jutting out anywhere to disrupt the lines of the dog. Use thinning shears to trim away any such hair.

Never clipper a smooth-coated breed. Clippering a smooth coat thickens the coat and may lighten the color. Furthermore, you run the risk of the new hair coming in curly or wavy. Why gamble ruining the coat of perhaps the best dog you ever bred? Learn to care for the coat properly before the wrong approach costs you a Best In Show.

Spitz Breeds

Spitz breeds, such as Samoyeds, Siberian Huskies, Shiba Inus, Keeshonden, and Pomeranians, have a dense double coat. The only way to keep such a coat in good condition is to keep it free of loose undercoat and to be constantly removing dead guard hair so that new coat is always coming in.

Figure 6-11: Alaskan Malamute

Figure 6-12: Keeshond

Every hair must be line-brushed against the lay, as with the drop-coated breeds. However, if the coat is short enough, it can be brushed with a slicker. For longer coats (2 inches or more in length), use a pin brush.

Too many people believe that brushing this type of coat will take out the undercoat, which will make the coat as a whole appear too thin. Actually, just the opposite is the case.

Figure 6-13: Samoyed

The more a spitz breed is properly brushed, the thicker its coat will be. As a judge, I am appalled when I examine a dog in the show ring that has a matted, packed undercoat. Remember, the welfare of our dogs should be our main priority.

Coated Breeds With a Jacket

These are the breeds that have hanging hair in some areas, but you want the "jacket," or torso coat, to lay smoothly and tightly over the body. Coated breeds with jackets include Golden Retrievers, Setters, Bernese Mountain Dogs, Papillons, Australian Shepherds, the Belgian herding breeds, and many more.

Chapter 6 / TRICKS OF THE TRADE

Figure 6-14: Long-Haired Dachshund

Figure 6-15: Papillion

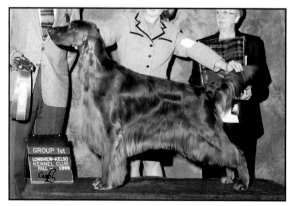

Figure 6-16: Irish Setter

For this type of coat, brush all furnishings against the lay, as with drop-coated breeds. Work the jacket with the lay, using a stripping knife as a comb, followed by a pumice stone. Both of these steps remove the dead hair, but in different layers.

Follow this procedure with one referred to as "packing the coat." For this step, you will need a blade brush (or a dense, natural-bristle brush on which all the bristles are the same length). There should be very little space between the rows of bristles, and the bristle surface must be flat. A flat surface is required for flattening and straightening the coat—any curve to the bristle surface will lift the coat.

Along with a blade brush, you will need a spray bottle of water (for coats that are bathed) or a spray bottle of rubbing alcohol (for coats that are pulled but not bathed) and a hand towel easily rolled up in your hand. Using a white towel will help keep you from returning dirt to the coat.

Wet the jacket from the appropriate spray bottle. Then, with the blade brush in one hand and the rolled-up towel in the other, alternate strokes along the lay of the jacket until the coat is completely dry and laying the way you want. Packing the jacket at least twice a week will control even the wildest of hair. Use a slicker on the feet and short-coated areas, and check for loose hair with a comb, just as you would do on a drop-coated breed.

Hard-Coated Breeds (Wire or Broken)

For any hair that must be pulled, you will need rubber fingers, stripping knives, a Dr. Scholl's Corn and Callous Remover, and a pumice stone. If you are a serious Terrier person, you may learn to pull hair almost entirely with your bare fingers, but beware the price your body may have to pay as you get older. Rubber fingers give you better traction, so you don't have to work as hard to pull hair, which makes the process easier on your hands, arms, and elbows.

There are many types of stripping knives of varying functions available for pulling wire or broken coats. (Check with your breed mentors to learn which knives are best for your breed and its coat type.) When you are pulling other coats, use a selection of knives. If you have a variety of knives available, you can switch back and forth, which will save your hand unnecessary strain and soreness.

When you are learning how to pull hair, I recommend using a Dr. Scholl's Corn and Callous Remover instead of a knife. You are less likely

Figure 6-17: Wire-Haired Dachshund

Figure 6-18: Giant Schnauzer

Figure 6-19: Cairn Terrier

to cut hair with this tool. As you get proficient, then buy your stripping knives.

The pumice stone is used to remove dead hair and undercoat, and it is used like a brush. Very little pressure is needed; just brush over the coat lightly. Done on a regular basis (once a week), this will help keep the coat in a steady state of growth and rejuvenation.

SCISSORING

With regard to scissoring, you must learn how to pick up scissors so that as you cut, only one blade is moving. This enables you to cut straighter lines. Put your little finger under the finger rest; put the next finger in the finger hole; then put the next two fingers under the edge of the scissors for balance. Your thumb slips into the thumb hole.

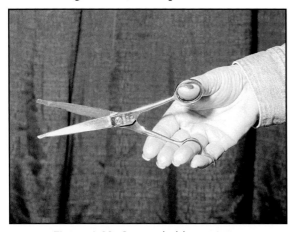

Figure 6-20: Correct hold on scissors

When you hold scissors in this manner, only the thumb moves, so only one blade moves. Make sure to keep just the tips of your finger and thumb in the holes, otherwise your hand loses leverage.

You need to handle scissors in order to know if they fit, and every pair fits a hand differently. Also, while learning to scissor, use average-quality scissors. With average quality, you have more chances to scissor over mistakes. With high-quality scissors, one chance to cut right is all you get. As you improve, improve the quality of scissors you buy.

As for thinning shears, it is best to get a pair that only has teeth on one of the blades. Double-sided thinning shears can cut chunks. Also, the fewer teeth (or the coarser the cutting blade), the finer the finish. Most thinning shears have approximately 44 teeth. I recommend a 32-tooth shear. The more teeth there are, the more scissor marks you will have on the coat. A 32-tooth shear takes more cutting time, but it leaves considerably fewer marks.

Keep a chunk of white chalk in with your scissors. The chalk absorbs moisture, so your scissors will stay sharp longer.

SHOW TIPS

Keep in mind that the objective is not to make most breeds look like they've been groomed to perfection but to make them look like nature has created perfection.

❖ **Buy only nylon nooses for your grooming arm.** Leather nooses can leave a dye ring on a wet dog. Flat-ribbed nooses are my favorite.

❖ **Refrain from clippering whiskers on a dog with a dark face, because clippering whiskers can make the dog's muzzle gray faster.** On dark faces, use only scissors to remove whiskers, if you want to remove the them. I don't believe any dog has ever won or lost on the status of its whiskers; however, make sure to check your breed standard to verify that removing whiskers is an acceptable practice.

❖ **A word about chalks:** It is legal to use chalks as long as you are using them for cleaning purposes, and you remove the chalk before showing. The best formula is one-half corn starch, one-quarter baby powder, and one-quarter of any of the commercial grooming powders. Corn starch alone does not stick to hair; baby powder alone is too silky and can be felt in a coat even after removal; commercial powders alone have to be bathed out or they damage the coat. The combination of all three, however, can't be felt, sticks to coat, and does not have to be washed out.

❖ **When bathing a dog that has stains, use only lukewarm water.** Cold or hot water can set stains. To remove grease from a coat, use liquid dish washing soap and cold water. (If the coat is extremely greasy, lather the coat with detergent or shampoo while the coat is dry.) Hot water dissolves the grease to where it soaks into the hair shaft and is still in the coat after you dry the dog. Cold water will bead up the grease so you can wash it off of the hair shaft.

Chapter 6 / TRICKS OF THE TRADE

❖ **One of the easiest ways to keep a white dog white is to use the laundry pre-wash product called Easy Wash.** Before you wet the dog down for a bath, rub Easy Wash into the white portions of the dirtiest or heavily-stained areas of the coat, then wet the dog and give the dog a bath. It will take one layer of staining off each time you use it, so using it each time you bathe the dog helps keep the coat white.

❖ **Boric acid powder, either dry or mixed with water to make a paste, can be used to remove stains.** It is particularly helpful in keeping face hair white and stain free.

❖ **If you are having problems with severe static,** Static Guard, or water mixed with a small measure of liquid fabric softener, sprayed lightly on your brush may help. Also, a satin crate pad cover eliminates most static.

❖ **Oil can be very damaging to hair if applied to a coat improperly.** Oil treatments are not for novice show groomers.

❖ **Practice your brushing technique.** The closer to the end of a brush handle you can hold a brush, the better job of brushing you will do.

❖ **Hair that is scissored tends to separate when the dog moves.** Hair that is pulled tends to cling to the surrounding hair.

❖ **When pulling hair, pull in the direction you want the hair to grow.** Pulling can affect the direction hair grows by turning the follicle in the direction you're pulling.

❖ **Try to work only the undercoat when attempting some "creative grooming."** Trying to hide anything about the dog by manipulating its top coat may actually draw attention to what you're trying to make unnoticeable.

❖ **Straggly hairs give the dog the appearance of being thin-coated.** Short and thick is better than long and straggly.

❖ **Always take nails back as far as possible before scissoring feet, then scissor only to the end of the nail.** If the nails show, the foot will give the appearance of being longer and flatter than it is.

❖ **Except on Poodles, never scissor between toes from underneath,** since this can adversely affect the tight look of the foot from the top. If the toes look separated, the foot will give the appearance of being flatter than it is.

❖ **If your breed standard allows it, remove the hair from around the large pad of the foot.** If that hair accumulates such things as mud, snow, feces, urine, etc, it can break the foot down.

❖ **Blue shampoo intensifies yellow stains.** Purple shampoo neutralizes yellowing.

Remember that grooming is an act of preventive health care, as well as a necessary piece of the whole package. Our first responsibility is to the health and well-being of our dogs. If we meet that responsibility, we enhance more than our show appearances.

Chapter 6 / TRICKS OF THE TRADE

*It makes no difference what you name your cat—
It never comes when you call it anyway.*

advertising dogs

Rick Rutledge was the original owner of the *Canine Chronicle*, the first weekly dog show magazine. The *Chronicle* had been publishing issues for a year or two, when the AKC board asked for Rick's attendance at one of their board meetings. At the meeting, the board said something to the effect that it disapproved of the *Chronicle*; they felt that it served only to attempt to influence AKC's judges.

This is one of those moments where a normal person thinks of a sharp reply a week after the fact. Rick told me later that he had no idea how his reply sprang to mind right there and then. He said to the board, "Gentlemen, if your judges judged dogs, I'd be out of business tomorrow."

The meeting ended, and the board never said another word about it to him. And Rick was right. No one would spend money on advertising if it didn't help. Therein lies the credence in the saying: "It pays to advertise." Considering the number and sizes of the all-breed publications available, it really must be true.

TARGET THE AUDIENCE

When advertising, first decide who you want to reach. It is the cornerstone of any advertising campaign—targeting the audience. Advertising is a waste of money and effort when it never comes to the attention of the right people.

If you are advertising stud dogs in an attempt to become a recognizable name in your breed or at least an impressive presence among your peers, stick with breed publications. If you are advertising for the sole purpose of selling puppies, be sure to advertise where new buyers are looking. If I were still breeding dogs and selling puppies, I would have an ad in the *AKC Gazette* every month, now that it is available on some newsstands.

The breed publications are great magazines. However, people who are new to the world of purebred dogs and shows are unaware of the existence of these publications (although the presence of the Internet in more people's home may be changing this). Therefore, unless you are a recognizable name in your breed, you probably will have less success in selling puppies through breed publications.

One editorial aside, if you will permit me. AKC, to the public, means quality. If AKC is going to maintain that reputation, it needs to do all in its power to prevent puppy mills from advertising in the *Gazette*. The effort is there. As I understand it, for instance, the *Gazette* will not accept ads from any USDA-licensed breeders. However, the AKC needs our help to stay on top of the situation. If you ever find a breeder's classified ad in the *Gazette* to be suspect, contact the publication directly. *Dog World* and *Dog Fancy* classified ads may very well include a high percentage of puppy mills. It would be a shame should the *AKC Gazette* develop that type of customer base.

Keep in mind that the AKC is only a registration body; it is not a police force. It has no right to refuse registration to any proven purebred puppies. On the other hand, the *AKC Gazette* has every right to ensure that its advertisers are responsible breeders dedicated to the quality, betterment, and well-being of their breeds.

Back to the topic at hand. I believe the main reason for advertising is to try to influence judges (or at least catch their eye). If that is your purpose, place your ads in the publications read by judges. The better the writers and articles, the greater the chances that judges are reading. The all-breed magazines are sent to the majority of the AKC judges. Then again, you can always ask some of your favorite judges which publications they read.

The breed magazines are very important to owners and breeders, but they are probably not the wisest use of your advertising dollars, if your purpose is to reach judges.

THE ADVERTISING BUDGET

The same things relevant to smart spending in the care and show preparation of our dogs applies to advertising our dogs. Figure out how much you can afford per year on advertising, then use that money to your best advantage.

If you buy a new Volvo and drive it off the lot, you are suddenly amazed by the number of Volvos you see on the road. Once we're associated with something, we notice it more.

If you have Akitas, you're going to take notice of all other Akitas you see in show magazines, but you might never notice the ads on toy breeds. If, however, you open up three consecutive issues of a magazine and see an ad for my Maltese in each one, you will most likely remember all of the ads, because the human mind generally remembers something after encountering it three consecutive times. This is known in the advertising world as a "recticular activating system." So the first thing to understand is that ads are most effective if they are run in units of three.

Second, use a different ad each time. If you use the exact same ad over and over, readers will think they've seen it before and pass over it. So use a different ad but have a theme or a similar layout or the same print style or logo—something that will identify the ads as being about the same dog.

AD LAYOUTS

Layout is paramount to successful advertising. The fewer words in an ad, the more likely it will be read. The more white space in an ad, the more likely it will be looked at—you only want necessary information. The exception is advertising in breed publications; in these ads, there is no such thing as too much information, and the information should always include the names of the sire, the dam, and the breeder.

The most important piece of ad information aimed at judges is the location where the dog is being shown. Take care, however. This piece of information requires subtlety. You want to let judges know in what area of the country the dog is being shown, without giving the impression of pushing your dog on judges' attentions. For example, if you are showing your own dog, provide not only your name (as owner-handler) but your address

Chapter 7 / TRICKS OF THE TRADE

as well. This will tell judges, in an unobtrusive way, where your dog is being shown.

Many judges think the tactic of saying specifically where the dog will be shown backfires. For example: "See you in Louisville." It comes across as pushy instead of informative. Trying to shove any portion of an ad down a judge's throat won't make points with your target audience. Advertising should entice, not offend.

Location is significant because advertising is more of an interest catcher than an influence. When I see an ad for a gorgeous Great Dane, for instance, I want to know what area of the country it's being shown in so that I can look for that Dane when I judge in that part of the country. That's not to say I will put the Dane up, but it will get a second look, because I'm keeping an eye out for it. (That's not politics—it's human nature.)

There are companies that specialize in dog show advertising, and they do a great job. They are expensive, though.

If you want help putting an advertising campaign together or are in the market for business cards or a logo or whatever, go to any local community college or university that has classes in advertising or layout or graphic arts, and meet with the instructor. Offer a prize of $50 or $100 for the student who comes up with the best idea for what you need. That way, you're getting 20 or 30 ideas as opposed to one idea from a company that could charge you as much as $500 for a logo. Students can come up with some great ideas, and most instructors love it because they like their students to work on practical projects.

AD PHOTOS

With ideas for layout in mind, determine what kinds of pictures you are going to use. When you're getting started, you can use informal shots in breed publications, but use only show photos in all-breed show magazines. Most people in this world (not just those in the dog world) are followers. If you want judges to take notice, you need to let them know that the dog is winning under a variety of judges. Hence, the sensible use of show photos.

Save your great photos for when your dog is a recognizable name. That is when you want your ads to be the most memorable.

Insofar as photos are concerned, make a copy of the photo you intend to use. It is important to know how it will reproduce in black and white or color and on the type of paper used by the magazine's printers.

Pay attention to what you're wearing when you show your dogs; we always do our best winning when we least expect it, so always be prepared. For black and white ads, avoid wearing red if you have dark-colored dogs, since red reproduces either black or dark gray. Refrain from wearing checks with smooth-coated dogs, because it will distort the topline of the dog in a photo. Forgo wearing patterns or prints with a parti-colored dog, because it will wash out the dog.

Always publish photos that put your dog in the best possible light. In other words, you want to use only photos that show off the dog's structural and breed strengths. Guaranteed, a bad photo will be interpreted as a lousy dog, not a lousy picture.

Never—and I mean absolutely never—alter a photograph in its print form to improve the look or quality of the dog. Ethics and integrity aside, the alteration may look fine as a photograph but will show as an altered photo when reproduced.

Finally, use photos in which all of the participants are looking at the dog. When all eyes are on the dog, the reader's eyes will automatically focus on the dog as well. In photos where the people are looking toward the camera, your eye is first going to focus on the person who is looking back at you.

The dog needs to be the center of attention in the ad. You can't always get everyone to look at the dog, but you can ask the photographer to request it of the people in the photo shoot.

ATTENTION TO STRATEGY

You expect too much if you try to advertise a dog into wins. Although judges may be intrigued by an ad, they will not be told what to do by advertisements. For instance, most judges have no appreciation for standards quoted in ads (as if the judge needs a lesson in standards).

Stick to advertising only what the dog has already accomplished. While you're building wins, keep your ads simple. Once you have some big wins under your belt, then is the time to advertise big, if you so choose. And keep your ads positive. Negative remarks about one's competition may be an accepted practice in political campaigns, but it is inappropriate when advertising dogs.

Remember to take a soft approach with your ads. You want to entice, not offend. Judges, like all of us, hate having their sensibilities treaded upon. Inform gently—perhaps with a touch of humor or elegance—dazzle with an excellent photo, but don't push.

RECAP

1. Determine who your target audience is.

2. Decide where you are going to advertise and how often, in accordance with your budget.

3. Select the right layout for your ad--keep it simple, with a signature characteristic that easily identifies the ad as yours.

4. Select photos that capture the best your dog can be.

No failure is ever final—nor is any success.

the breeder's integrity

Breeding dogs does not necessarily make one a breeder. Being a good breeder involves dedication to the constant improvement of your particular breed of dog.

Planning and protecting the future of your breed is what will make you a breeder. The basics of a healthy, sound dog is top priority and your first responsibility as a breeder. Your next responsibility is to breed in accordance with your breed standard—not for what you like or what fashion may be winning for the moment, but for what your standard calls. With the rising lobbies against dog breeding in this country, responsible breeding is the first best hope for staving off the potential onslaught of breeding prohibitions.

Again, to be a good breeder, read your breed standard. Study it, understand it, and breed for quality, not quantity. There are enough dogs in the world already. To breed dogs just for selling stock is almost criminal—and I'm not referring to traditional puppy mills.

If you want to be a good breeder, you have to be responsible for the dogs you breed throughout the whole of their lives. You must also make the hard decisions, such as putting puppies down that are incapable of dealing with and living in our world, as well as spaying or neutering dogs that most likely would produce unsound puppies.

With very few exceptions, I am opposed to repeat breedings, because we should always breed for improvement. When we repeat a breeding, all we are doing is duplicating what we've already done. If quality and improvement are not your first concerns in breeding, give up breeding—for the sake

Chapter 8 / TRICKS OF THE TRADE

Figure 8-01: Sporting Group—English Setter

Figure 8-02: Hound Group—
Scottish Deerhound

of your breed.

I also believe dogs should be bred to fit their breed standards instead of rewriting standards to fit the dogs being bred. Knowing your breed standard is the first best step to breeding or showing. Judging is a subjective activity, and breed standards are open to interpretation, but all of us need parameters within which to begin and proceed in this sport. Breed standards and AKC rules are the fundamentals of our sport. Remember, however, that nothing in our sport is black and white. All you can do is the best you can do for your breed and your sport.

Health problems are becoming so severe that we must pay more attention to what we're doing and how we're breeding or be willing to forfeit the right to breed dogs in this country. If you are having any kind of problem in any part of the genetic health of your dogs, go to the experts (see listing in the Resources section of this book). Don't try to figure it out with your next-door neighbor or your general-practice veterinarian. Go to those who know the most, the people who are doing the research. None of us can reduce the instances of genetic problems until we learn what the problems are. Only then can we learn how to deal with these problems (and learn, we must).

Research what is acceptable and what is illegal in the enhancing and altering of dogs. Remember the primary objective of conformation showing is to help determine the best quality for breeding. If you spend time and money fixing the appearance of a dog at the expense of breeding quality, you are simply creating the illusion of quality. That is not what the sport intended, and if you lose sight of the intention, you risk your own integrity as a breeder.

The breeders who know what problems their specific breeds are prone to are the breeders who have fewer problems, because they learn how to prevent them. Problem prevention begins with a thorough knowledge of our dogs. There is no excuse for not knowing your dogs in detail, including such things as the number of teeth, condition of the testicles, and range of temperaments in each litter. It is my opinion that if a dog is not equipped to function as a dog, it is not a whole animal. Our responsibility is to breed whole, healthy animals.

The longer you are in dogs, the more you will find value in using an overlay of the physical structure of a dog. Start with the full structure, then be able to peel away one layer at a time. This is an invaluable tool for the breeder as well as the exhibitor.

Always bear in mind that it is a breeder's responsibility to breed with the consideration that the dog must be capable of doing what it was originally bred to do. If a Herding dog is incapable physically or temperamentally of herding, a Hound or Sporting dog of hunting, a Terrier of going to ground, etc, it should be spayed or neutered. But as responsible breeders, we should do all we can to minimize the chance of bringing such a dog into this world.

Also, as breeders it is our responsibility to place dogs in appropriate homes. The dog has to fit its owner's lifestyle and activities. Is it right to sell a puppy with structural weaknesses to a person who wants a dog as a long-distance running companion? It is a bad match for the puppy and for the prospective owner.

I am constantly dumbfounded by the number of breeders who think that their "pet" puppies can be sold to obedience homes. Homes looking for a dog to work or do obe-

Figure 8-03: Working Group—Doberman Pinscher

Chapter 8 / TRICKS OF THE TRADE

Figure 8-04: Terrier Group—Scottish Terrier

dience require dogs with the most sound structure. A dog that falls short of its breed type but has exquisitely sound structure may be the best choice for these homes.

If prospective owners are looking for something that would be found more readily in another breed, suggest that breed and save you, them, and your puppies the heartache of a bad match.

Finally, take care to plan your breeding program. If you are breeding to make money, you cannot afford to be as careful as you ought to be in developing a breeding program. Breeding is ideally an effort of love and should not be a commercial venture. It is an expensive endeavor, but the return on investment must be in quality, not in capital. Consider your motive before you proceed, and for the sake of the dog world, make sure you are breeding dogs for the right reason.

In your breeding program, then, breed for total quality. The body has to be balanced; balance means all pieces function together as one whole. The dog has to be a good mix of structural soundness and breed-specific capabilities, along with good health and proper type and temperament.

When buyers take one of your puppies home, whether they pay for a show prospect or a pet, their confidence in buying from a breeder instead of from a pet store is in your hands, as are the lives of the dogs your breeding program has produced. It is up to you to help challenge the attitude of people who swear they will only have mixed breeds because there are too many problems that come with a purebred dog.

Figure 8-05: Toy Group—Chihuahua

THE BREEDER'S INTEGRITY / Chapter 8

Figure 8-06: Non-Sporting Group—Dalmatian

Figure 8-07: Herding Group—Cardigan Welsh Corgi

To each prospective buyer, you represent all breeders. It is a sobering responsibility to carry–puppies and people are depending on your integrity, best intentions, and willingness to keep learning.

Chapter 8 / TRICKS OF THE TRADE

Excuses are your lack of faith in your own power.

AKC rules and ethics

According to the *AKC Bulletin* published in November 1989, the regulations regarding alterations to show dogs come down to this: If you do anything to a dog to alter its appearance from what it might have been if you had not done the alteration, it is illegal.

The best rule you can follow is to breed carefully instead of breeding to whatever and fixing the result. Also, be aware of what surgical procedures are acceptable and unacceptable for show. AKC has established a list of acceptable surgical procedures. It is a good idea to know what they are and the fines and suspensions associated with those procedures that are unacceptable.

AKC has a rule book for every show event, be it conformation, obedience, den and herding trials, or any of the myriad other activities you can

Figure 9-01: Golden Retriever—Obedience

Figure 9-02: Newfoundland—Water Trial

Chapter 9 / TRICKS OF THE TRADE

Figure 9-03: Alaskan Malamute—Weight Pulling

Figure 9-04: Labrador Retriever—Water Retrieve

get involved in with your dog. A good habit to get into is to always have with you every rule book that applies to every event in which you and your dogs are competing.

Moreover, keep in mind that AKC does not write the breed standards–parent clubs write breed standards. If you have a problem with your breed's standard, look to your parent club. AKC is not to blame. If you are unhappy with what your parent club does, then get involved and try to make things better. Just complaining about what's wrong never helps anyone, including yourself.

If you have a measurable or weighable breed (a breed with a height or weight disqualification for conformation), be sure you know the rules, as well as your dog's measurements or weight. There is no excuse for an exhibitor or handler to be ignorant of his or her dog's size.

Know how to measure and weigh your dog correctly. Judges are taught at seminars, but breeders and owners should be the first to know. If you have any questions about measuring or weighing, contact your local AKC representative for assistance.

Both the measuring wickets and the scale must be set by the judge, but make sure you check them yourself. The dog must be measured in a normal show stance. If you have a breed that is stacked on a table, measuring must take place on the table. If you have a breed that is stacked on the floor, measuring must take place on the floor.

Weighing accurately is more difficult, due to the fact that there is a variety of weighing equipment used.

If a dog is found to be ineligible for its class or division, it must be excused. If the breed standard dictates a disqualification for height or weight and the dog does not fit within the standard, then the dog must be disqualified. A dog that has been disqualified thus by three different judges may not be shown again.

Know what products and procedures are illegal to use on show dogs. My personal belief is that any product or procedure that alters or masks the genetic foundation of a dog is wrong—period—end of story. The AKC rule is: Any alteration that changes the appearance of a dog makes the dog ineligible for show.

All breed standards override AKC rules. Therefore, it is legal to crop ears, dock tails, and remove dewclaws, in accordance with specific breed standards. Some breed standards even allow for honorable scars.

I do not advocate using anything that misrepresents the true genetic makeup of a dog. It cheats the sport and hurts our breeds.

When it comes to AKC rules generally, anyone who is going to show dogs will encounter debate and conflicting views. Know now that interpretations and perceptions will vary. Judges barely have time to judge the dogs; they have no time to police the particular practices of each exhibitor.

Nothing about showing dogs is comfortably black and white, and the faster you understand it, the faster you can let go of that expectation and enjoy the experience more fully. If you see a specific problem surfacing in your breed, your best option is to raise the issue with your parent club. That's where changes can really begin.

As for exhibiting, preparation and presentation choices are yours alone. The choices you make may or may not have negative consequences, but consider this: Each person who prepares and presents a dog with reasonable honesty enriches the sport, win or lose. And all who walk away with a Best in Show through integrity, hard work, and careful breeding enrich the breed they show.

There's a PHA handler up in the Northwest who has a saying that I absolutely love: "Show your dog to its best advantage without taking advantage of anybody else." So do what it takes to show your dog in the best possible light—show the judge the best your dog can be. Remember, you paid

Chapter 9 / TRICKS OF THE TRADE

the same amount for your entry as everyone else. Get your money's worth, but not at someone else's expense.

As members of the sport of purebred dogs, all we can do is the best we can do, and try to share what we know. Be a mentor to beginners coming up behind you. Teach what you can and keep your mind open to new information. Nothing remains static, so we harm ourselves, our breeds, and our sport by standing still.

Thoughtfully advance. Dare to be a good example.

resources

MAGAZINES

AKC Gazette
260 Madison Ave
New York NY 10016-2401
(212) 696-8200
Subscriptions: 1 (800) 533-7323

Canine Chronicle
3622 NE Jackson Rd
Ocala FL 34479
(352) 369-1104

Dogs in Review
PO Box 30430
Santa Barbara CA 93130
(805) 692-2045

Dog News
1115 Broadway
New York NY 10010
(212) 807-7100 ext. 588

Showsights
8848 Beverly Hills
Lakeland FL 33809-1604
(941) 858-3839

ASSOCIATIONS

Owner Handlers Association (OHA)
Rose Robischon
1100 Ridgebury Rd
New Hampton NY 10958
(914) 374-2708
Website: http://www.prodogs.com/OHA

Professional Handlers Association (PHA)
Mailing Address:
15810 Mt. Everest Ln
Silver Springs MD 20906
(301) 924-0089

Professional Handlers Certification Board (CPH)
Kathy Bowser
15810 Mt. Everest Ln
Silver Springs MD 20906
(301) 924-0089

Jane Flowers
413 Dempsey Ave, SW
Buffalo MN 55313
(612) 682-3366

American Dog Owners Association (ADOA)
Mailing Address:
1654 Columbia Turnpike
Castleton NY 12033

CANINE HEALTH

Brucellosis
Antech – Diagnostics
13633 N. Cave Creek Rd
Phoenix AZ 85022
(602) 971-4110
FAX: (602) 225-0439

Diagnostic Lab
College of Veterinary Medicine
Cornell University
Ithaca NY 14853-6401
(607) 253-3900
FAX: (607) 253-3943

Canine Reproduction
Dr. Robert van Hutchinson
Animal Clinic Northview
34910 Center Ridge Rd
North Ridgeview OH 44039
(440) 327-8282

Resources / TRICKS OF THE TRADE

Cardiac Conditions
American College of Veterinary Internal
Medicine--Cardiology
7175 W. Jefferson Ave, Ste 2125
Lakewood CO 80235-2320
(800) 245-9081
FAX: (303) 980-7136

Cardiac Conditions
Dr. David Sisson
University of Illinois
School of Veterinary Medicine
2001 S. Lincoln
Urbana IL 61801
(217) 333-5324 or (217) 333-5300
FAX: (217) 244-1475

Dr. Matt Miller
Texas A & M School of Veterinary Medicine
College Station TX 77843-4474
(409) 845-2351
FAX: (409) 845-6978

Canine Eye Registration Foundation (CERF)
SCC-A
Purdue University
1235 SCC-A
West Lafayette IN 47907-1235
(317) 494-8179
FAX: (317) 494-9918

Deafness
Dr. George Strain
School of Veterinary Medicine
Communication Sciences & Disorders
Louisiana State University
Baton Rouge LA 70803

DNA
VetGen Canine Genetic Services
3728 Plaza Dr, Ste 1
Ann Arbor MI 48108
(800) 483-8436 or (734) 669-8440
FAX: (734) 669-8441

The Deubler Genetic Disease Testing Lab
University of Pennsylvania
(215) 898-3375
FAX: (215) 573-2162

PE AgGen
1756 Picasso Ave
Davis CA 95616
1 (800) 362-3644

Stormont Laboratories
1237 E. Beamer St, Ste A
Woodland CA 95695
(916) 661-3078
FAX: (916) 661-0391

Genetic Disease Control (GDC)
Institute for Genetic Disease Control
 in Animals
PO Box 222
Davis CA 95617
(916) 756-6773

GRF Skin Diseases
Genetic Skin Disorders
1635 Grange Hall Rd
Dayton OH 45432

Hip Dysplasia
PennHip
c/o Synbiotics Corporation
1 (800) 228-4305

Orthopedic Foundation for Animals (OFA)
Dr. Greg Keller, Executive Director
2300 Nifong Blvd
Columbia MO 65201-3856
(573) 442-0418
FAX: (573) 875-5073

Dr. Barclay Slocum, DVM
621 River Ave
Eugene OR 97404
(541) 689-9393

Metabolism
Screening Lab for Inborn Errors of Metabolism
The Section of Medical Genetics
School of Veterinary Medicine
University of Pennsylvania
Philadelphia PA 19104

Mouth Problems
Dr. Edward Eisner, DVM
Diplomate, AVDC
2178 S. Colorado Blvd
Denver CO 80222
(303) 757-8481

Poison
National Animal Poison Control Center
1 (800) 548-2432
(900) 680-0000

Progressive Retinal Atrophy (PRA)
PRA Research
 James A. Baker Institute for Animal Health
Cornell University
College of Veterinary Medicine
Hungerford Hill Rd
Ithaca NY 14853-6401
(607) 256-5600
FAX: (607) 256-5608

Thyroid
College of Veterinary Medicine
Michigan State University
Attention: Vet Diagnostic Lab
PO Box 30076
Lansing MI 48909-7576
(517) 353-0621

School of Veterinary Medicine
University of California at Davis
Davis CA 95616

NY State College of Veterinary Medicine
Diagnostic Laboratory
Cornell University
Ithaca NY 14853-6401
(607) 253-3673

To transport dogs to other countries, especially to Australia, the following labs can be helpful:

Brucellosis
ME Tube Agglutination Test
National Veterinary Services Laboratories
1800 Dayton Rd
Ames IA 50010
(515) 239-8266

Ehrlichia Canis
Immofluorescent Antibody Test
Oklahoma Animal Disease
Diagnostic Laboratory
Oklahoma State University
PO Box 7001
Stillwater OK 74076-7001
(405) 744-6623
FAX: (405) 744-8612

Leptospirosis
Agglutination Test
Texas Veterinary Medical
Diagnostic Laboratory
Drawer 3040
College Station TX 77841-3040
or
1 Sippel Rd
College Station TX 77843
(409) 845-3414

Rabies Anitbody Titer
Rapid Fluorescent Focus Inhibition Test
RFFIT
Department of Veterinary Diagnosis
Veterinary Medical Center
Kansas State University
Manhattan KS 66506-5600
(785) 532-4483

RECOMMENDED READING AND OTHER MEDIA

"Better Breeding Column," *AKC Gazette*, Pat Craige Trotter and Cindy Vogels.

Bites, Breath & Benevolent Breeding, Edward Eisner DVM, 4th edition, 1994.
    Call (303) 757-8481.

Born to Win, Patricia Craig, Doral Publishing, 1997.

Canine Reproduction - A Breeder's Guide, Dr. Phyllis A. Holst, Alpine Publications, 1985.

Canine Terminology, Harold Spira, Howell Book House, 1982.
    This book is out of print; however, try used-book stores.

The Doberman Pinscher CD, Sherluck Multimedia, 1996.
    Call (800) 662-4118 or (253) 631-1442.
    (CDs on other breeds are also available from Sherluck Multimedia.)

The Dog in Action, McDowell Lyon, Howell Book House, 1950.

Dog Locomotion and Gait Analysis, Curtis M. Brown, Hoflin Publications, 1986.

Dog Steps, Rachel Page Elliott, Howell Book House, 1973.
    This is both a book and a video.

Hill's Atlas of Veterinary Clinical Anatomy, Veterinary Medicine Publishing Co., 1989.
    This book is available through:
    Mary Whittaker - Hill's Pet Nutrition, PO Box 148,
    Topeka KS 66601-0148. Call (913) 368-5588
    or contact voice mail at (800) 258-2403, ext 5588.

K-9 Structure & Terminology, Edward M. Gilbert Jr. and Thlema Brown, Howell Book House, 1995.

Puppy Puzzle: The Hastings Approach to Evaluating the Structural Quality of Puppies,
    Bob and Pat Hastings and Erin Rouse, Dogfolk Enterprises, 1998.
    Call (800) 967-3188 or log on to www.dogfolk.com to order.

Successful Dog Breeding, Chris Walkowicz and Bonnie Wilcox DVM, Prentice Hall Press, 1987.

UC Davis School of Veterinary Medicine Book of Dogs, Harper Collins Publishers, 1995.

table of visuals

1/ FIRST THINGS FIRST
1-01 Kennel lead... 18
1-02 Kennel lead in use 18
1-03 High cross-beam...................................... 19
1-04 Low cross-beam 19
1-05 Wishbone legs 19
1-06 Correctly grooved surface........................ 20
1-07 Incorrectly grooved surface..................... 20
1-08 Grooming arm with appendage in place.. 21
1-09 Grooming arm with appendage folded..... 21

2/ PUPPY EVALUATIONS
2-01 Correct hold for evaluating temperament.. 27
2-02 Correct hold for suspended position....... 28
2-03 Correct front hold for suspended position .. 28
2-04 Correct rear hold for suspended position .. 28
2-05 Suspended position 29
2-06 Standing position 29
2-07 Check height at shoulder 30
2-08 In relation to length of body.................... 30
2-09 Check depth of body 30
2-10 In relation to height of leg 30
2-11 Zygomatic arch from side 34
2-12 Zygomatic arch from front 35
2-13 Simulated growth plate at inside corner of eye........... 35
2-14 Proper occlusion 35
2-15 Improper occlusion.................................. 35
2-16 Good neck 36
2-17 Short neck 36
2-18 Good front assembly 37
2-19 Poor front assembly 37
2-20 Good reach.. 37
2-21 Short reach.. 37
2-22 Good neck 38
2-23 Ewe neck 38
2-24 Front-assembly equidistance................... 38
2-25 Good shoulders 39
2-26 High shoulders 39
2-27 Good depth of chest 40
2-28 Herring gut.. 40
2-29 Rear-assembly equidistance 41

Table of Visuals / TRICKS OF THE TRADE

	2-30 Proper rear assembly	42
	2-31 Sickle hocks	42
	2-32 U-shaped pelvis	43
	2-33 V-shaped pelvis	43
	2-34 Cow hocks from rear	43
	2-35 Open hocks from rear	43
	2-36 Good hocks from rear	44
	2-37 Good hocks from side	44
	2-38 Slipped hocks from side	44
3/	**NUTRITION**	
	3-01 Chinese Shar-Pei in good weight	52
	3-02 Chinese Shar-Pei underweight	52
	3-03 Chinese Shar-Pei overweight	52
4/	**TEACHING A DOG TO LEARN**	
5/	**DOG WHEREWITHAL**	
	5-01 Short nails, sound foot	70
	5-02 Foot damaged by long nails	70
	5-03 Afghan Hound—Lure coursing	72
	5-04 German Shepherd Dog—Obedience	72
	5-05 Chesapeake Bay Retriever—Field trial	72
	5-06 Siberian Huskies—Sledding	72
	5-07 Crate fan	79
	5-08 Chokes: nylon, obedience chain, snake chain	81
	5-09 Adjusting collar position	81
	5-10 Setting collar position	81
	5-11 Show lead, blade snap, and bolt snap	82
	5-12 Homemade dog bed	87
6/	**GROOMING FOR SHOW AND HEALTH**	
	6-01 Dog nail from underside	97
	6-02 Rake, pin brush, slicker, stainless steel comb, and blade brush	100
	6-03 Pumice stone, rubber fingers, and assorted stripping knives	100
	6-04 Drop-coated breed: Shih Tzu	102
	6-05 Drop-coated breed: Yorkshire Terrier	102
	6-06 Drop-coated breed: Afghan Hound	102
	6-07 Line-brushing	103
	6-08 Smooth-coated breed: Dalmatian	103

6-09	Smooth-coated breed: Great Dane 104
6-10	Smooth-coated breed: Doberman Pinscher 104
6-11	Spitz breed: Alaskan Malamute. 105
6-12	Spitz breed: Keeshond 105
6-13	Sptiz breed: Samoyed. 105
6-14	Coated breed with jacket: Long-Haired Dachshund 106
6-15	Coated breed with jacket: Papillon 106
6-16	Coated breed with jacket: Irish Setter. 106
6-17	Hard-coated breed: Wire-Haired Dachshund. 107
6-18	Hard-coated breed: Giant Schnauzer 107
6-19	Hard-coated breed: Cairn Terrier 107
6-20	Correct hold on scissors 108

7/ ADVERTISING DOGS

8/ THE BREEDER'S INTEGRITY

8-01	Sporting Group—English Setter 120
8-02	Hound Group—Scottish Deerhound 120
8-03	Working Group—Doberman Pinscher 121
8-04	Terrier Group—Scottish Terrier 122
8-05	Toy Group—Chihuahua. 122
8-06	Nonsporting Group—Dalmatian 123
8-07	Herding Group—Cardigan Welsh Corgi 123

9/ AKC RULES AND PERSONAL INTEGRITY

9-01	Golden Retriever—Obedience 125
9-02	Newfoundland—Water trial. 125
9-03	Alaskan Malamute—Weight pulling 126
9-04	Labrador Retriever—Water retrieve. 126

index

Acid milk 85
Adult structural soundness 68-73
Advertising
    audience 113-114, 118
    budget 115, 118
    layouts 115-116, 118
    photos 116-117, 118
    strategy 117-118
Air travel 78-80
Aloe vera 88
Alterations 125
American Dog Owners Association
    (ADOA) 80, 129
American Kennel Club (AKC)
    as a registration body 114
    board 113
    judges 113-118
    representative 126
    rules and regulations 120, 125-128
    shows 92
Animal husbandry 24
Arm, grooming
    appendage 20-21
    hinged 20-21
    motion in 20
    noose 109
Arthritis 45-46, 53
Attitude
    evaluating 46-47
    honing for show 84

Baiting
    in show circumstances 82-84
    in teaching circumstances 59-60
    with liver 82-84
Bathing 98-99
Behavior
    canine 55-59, 61-63, 67, 68-69
    human 55-63
    imprinting 56
Benkin, Priscilla 80
Bibliography, selected 132
Bite 35
Blade brush 99-100, 106
Bones
    assessing density 47
    balance 38, 41

between hip and tailset 46
    growth rate of 25, 31
    neck vertebrae 36
    spinal projection of 45
Boric acid 110
Breed standards
    disqualifications 127
    in breeding programs 119-123
    in conformation showing 127
    in evaluations 24, 29, 41, 46
Breeders
    responsibilities of 119-123, 125
Breeding
    evaluations to improve 25-26, 32
    for structure 23, 32, 42, 46, 47-48
    for type 23
    goal 23
    repeat 119-120
Brucellosis 129, 131

Calcium 51
Canadian Kennel Club (CKC) 91
Canine
    anatomy 24
    behavior 55-59, 61-63, 67, 68-69
    Eye Registration Foundation
        (CERF) 130
    reproduction 129
    structure 68-73
Cardiac conditions 130
Carpet fresheners 88
Cedar chips 87
Chalks 109
Chamois 103-104
Charcoal tablets 90
Chewing on wood 90
Chlorophyll tablets 89
Choke chains
    as a teaching tool 80-82
    how to use 81-82
    types of 81, 82
Clippering 104, 109
Conditioners 98
Cook, Dr. Janet 53
Cornell University 51
Crate fans 77-79
Crates 78-80, 84

Deafness 130
Dishes 86
Diuretic 76
DNA testing 24
Dog beds, outdoor 86-87
Dr. Scholl's Corn and Callous
    Remover 107-108
Dryers 99

Easy Wash 110
Education 25, 70, 71, 92-93, 95-96, 123, 128
Ehrlichia canis 131
Engel, Dr. Hal 24
Ensure 53
Evaluating for
    adult structural soundness 68-69
    attitude 46-47
    bone density 47
    decisions 32-48, 66
    home placement 48, 68-69
    nutritional effects 31, 50
    structural quality 23-24, 27-31, 47-48
    temperament 23, 27, 32-33
Evaluation
    procedure 24-32
        age of puppies 25
        consistency 27
        grading system 25-26, 27
Ewe neck 38, 72
Exercise pens 76-77, 85
Exercising 75

Feeding 51
    "lite" foods 53
Flies 86

Genetic temperament traits 32-33
Genetics 24, 45, 70-71, 98, 120, 130
Grooming
    agility and obedience dogs 95-96
    coated breeds with jackets 105-107
    drop-coated breeds 99, 101-103
    hard-coated breeds 100, 107-108
    smooth-coated breeds 99, 103-104
    spitz breeds 104-105
Grooming arm, selecting 20
    (see also Arms, grooming)
Grooming table, selecting 18-20
    (see also Tables, grooming)
Grooming tools

blade brush 99-100, 106
chalks 109
chamois 103-104
clippers 104, 109
Dr. Scholl's Corn and Callous
    Remover 107-108
hand towels 106
pin brush 99-100, 101-103, 105
pumice stone 100, 103-104, 106-108
rake 100
rubber fingers 100, 107
scissors 108-109
slicker 99-100, 101, 103, 105, 107
spray bottles 102, 106
stainless steel comb 99-100, 103
stripping knives 100, 106-108
thinning shears 104, 108
Growth plates 31, 34-35, 49

Hair follicles 98-99, 100
Hand towels 106
Handling classes 60-61
Head 33-34
Herring gut 40, 72
Hip dysplasia 45, 53, 130
Hocks 42-45, 70-71
    barrel 43-44
    cow 43-44
    open 43-44
    sickle 42, 72
    slipped 44-45, 53, 70-71
    spread 43-44
Humidifiers 88

Kennel leads 18
    (see also Leads, kennel)
Knees 43, 71
    (see also Patellas, luxating)

Lactinex 53
Leads
    for teaching 59, 82
    kennel 18
    show 82, 92
    types of snaps on 82
Leptospirosis 131
Lick sores 89
Line-brushing 102-103, 105
Litters
    color-marking 66-67

Litters (continued)
    keeping syblings 65-66
    naming 85
Liver bait 82-84

Magazines (see Publications)
Matching 76-77
Metabolism 131
Mirror
    used for evaluations 26
    used for grooming 99
    used for teaching 56
Mouth 35, 131

Nail
    care 96-97
    grinder 96-97
Neck 36-38
Novice exhibitor 91-93
Nutrition, puppy 49-51

Obesity 53-54
Occlusion 35
Oil treatments 110
Orthodontics 35
Owner Handlers Association
    (OHA) 129

Pacing 59
Parent clubs 126, 127
Patellas, luxating 43, 71
Pedigrees 25
Pediolyte 78
Pelvis
    tipped 46
    U-shaped 42
    V-shaped 42
Pin brush 99-100, 101-103, 105
Pine products 88
Poison 131
Pooper scoopers 85
Powder 103
Professional Handlers Association
    (PHA) 127
Professional Handlers Certification Board
    (CPH) 129
Progressive retinal atrophy (PRA) 131
Publications
    AKC Bulletin 125
    AKC Gazette 114

    all-breed 114, 116
    breed 114, 116
    Canine Chronicle 113, 129
    Dog Fancy 114
    Dog News 129
    Dog World 114
    Dogs in Review 129
    Showsights 129
Pumice stone 100, 103-104, 106-108
Puppies
    bottle-feeding vs tubing 67
    toys for 67
Puppy mills 114, 119

Rabies antibody titer 131
Rake 100
Recticular activating system 115
Road work 74-75
Rubber fingers 100, 107
Rutledge, Rick 113
RV travel 86

Scissoring 108-109, 110, 111
Scissors 108-109
Shampoos 98-99
Showing 90-94
Skunk odor 87-88
Slicker 99-100, 101, 103, 105, 107
Socialization 60-61
Spray bottles 102, 106
Stacking for show 90-91
Stainless steel comb 99-100, 103
Stains, removing 109, 110, 111
States Kennel Club (SKC) 91
Static 20, 82, 101-102, 110
Stewarding 93
Stripping knives 100, 106-108
Structure
    balance 45, 47
    compensation 45, 47
    consequences of poor 68-73
Supplements 50-52

Tables, grooming
    cross-beam on 19, 63
    for assessing condition 74
    for conformation showing 126
    for grooming 96, 99, 101-102
    for teaching 56-57, 58-59, 61, 62-63
    legs on 19

Tables, grooming (continued)
    motion in 19
    stacking on 90-91
    surfaces of 20, 63
Thinning shears 104, 108
Thyroid 131
Toenails 70, 96-97
    (see also Nail, care)

United Kennel Club (UKC) 91
Urine odor 89-90

Vanilla extract 89
Veterinarians 73-74
Vitamin C 51
Vocabulary, teaching dogs 60

Water buckets 76, 85
Weight
    excessive 52-54
    healthy 52
    increasing 53
    maintaining 52
Whiskers 109
Wickets 126

Zygomatic arch 33-34